THE LOST
The Story of A

NEW AND REVISED EDITION 2007

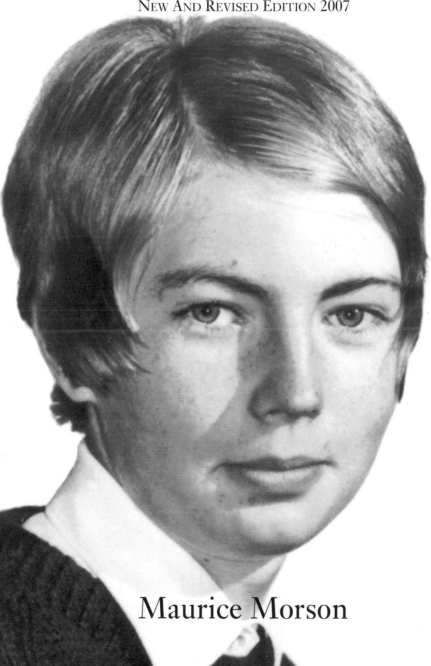

Maurice Morson

First edition 1995
Revised edition 2007

PUBLISHED BY REDBRIDGE BOOKS

© Maurice Morson 2007

British Library Cataloguing In Publication Data
A catalogue record for this book is available from the British Library.

ISBN 978–0–9520192–6–8

Typeset in 11pt Ehrhardt

Designed and printed in England by
Barnwell's Print Ltd, Printing Works
2-6 Penfold Street, Aylsham, Norfolk, NR11 6ET
Telephone: +44 (0)1263 732767

This book is dedicated to the memory of April Fabb and to those who wait and wonder

Life is the art of drawing sufficient
conclusions from insufficient premises

Samuel Butler (1835–1902)

By the same author: A City's Finest
The Lost Years (1995)
A Force Remembered
Rough Justice
Norwich Murders
Norfolk Mayhem and Murder

Contents

	Page
Acknowledgements	6
Forewords	8
Prologue	10
Illustrations	12
A Notice and a Country Place	14
A Farewell and a Cycle Ride	26
Viewed in a Very, Very Serious Light	38
Someone, Somewhere, Knows	49
If I saw a Battleship Upside Down in a Field	62
If Only There Were News	75
Sharing Other Tragedies	86
The Changing Times	97
The Evil That Men Do	108
Sufficient Conclusions From Insufficient Premises	119
Epilogue	129
Appendix	133
Index	135

Acknowledgements

Many people, official and unofficial, contributed to the two editions of this book. Some were special to the first edition (1995) and others came newly to this 2007 edition. Some have, of course, been special to both editions. Whoever, whenever and wherever the assistance came from I am grateful. I hope you will all accept that you have been remembered and thanked in this broadside of gratitude.

To some there must be a record of special thanks for without them I would not be presenting this new attempt to profile and solve the long running mystery of April Fabb.

I extend my gratitude to the officers, present and past, of the Norfolk Constabulary who gave up their time and expertise, particularly the officer currently having charge of the April Fabb investigation, Detective Superintendent Chris Hobley. His assistance has been invaluable and I wish him and his officers every success.

Eight Norfolk chief constables have been in post since 1969. The eighth, Mr Ian McPherson, came newly to Norfolk and the April Fabb mystery in 2007. He has allowed a long retired officer unfettered access to case records, exhibits and serving officers, sanctioning the provision of copies of documents, photographs and up to date information, and authorising publication of the same. His co-operation has been vital and is greatly appreciated. His keenness, and that of his officers, demonstrates that there is no time closure upon the April Fabb mystery.

In recognising the unreserved assistance of the police I stress that nothing within this book has been influenced by the Norfolk Constabulary or its authority, and any analysis or view that might be expressed is not attributable to the force or any representative of the force.

The inspiration of the local press is a powerful tool in a major investigation and their records are a valuable aid to research. The assistance given by staff of Archant Ltd [*Eastern Daily Press* and *Eastern Evening News*] is greatly appreciated and I thank Archant for permission to reproduce reports and photographs. In major enquiries the national press also have a role to play and I thank staff of *The Observer* for their assistance, particularly their representative in 1972, Anthony Peagam, who supplied and gave permission for the publication of photographs taken by him.

Photographs that have not been credited are author or family related.

To the Fabb family, mother, father (sadly now deceased) and daughters [April's sisters] who have grieved so long, I once again record my humble appreciation and admiration for the way you have conducted yourselves over so many years, and for voluntarily re-opening the wounds of yesteryear in agreeing to this new edition of your personal tragedy; but as you have said – those wounds have never closed. Neither the 1995 nor 2007 book would have been written without your support, which was given knowing the additional heartache that decision would bring. Thirty-eight years on you still co-operate and speak of what your family was, knowing that it can never be again. Only knowledge can now assuage what you have lost. As I and others said in 1995, repeated in 2007 – may you one day be rewarded.

Maurice Morson
September 2007

Forewords

pril's nephew, Duncan was 10 months old in 1969 when April disappeared.

Duncan is married now and his own child is growing up, not knowing of the anxious years which have gone before.

The harrowing emptiness in the life of a caring family and the added strain of the countless years of 'not knowing', is too difficult to contemplate.

The quiet dignity and fortitude of Mr and Mrs Fabb and their family, touched everyone on the enquiry at Metton and deepened their resolve to find April.

Sadly, the officers given the task in 1969 to find April, have long since retired – their search in vain.

The detailed research by Maurice Morson and the outline of subsequent enquiries, confirm that the search will continue and will not end, until it is known and the question has been answered – *"What has happened – to APRIL FABB?"*

R.Lester QPM
Detective Chief Superintendent (Rtd)
February 1995

It is nearly 40 years since April Fabb disappeared from her home in rural Norfolk, and the world now is very different from the one she would have known at age 13, when she disappeared.

One thing that will remain unchanged however, is the shock of a rural community at losing one of its residents, and the grief that April's family and friends have had to live with for nearly four decades. The courage and dignity of April's family in the face of such a personal loss, and such intense media interest, should not be underestimated, and indeed should be admired by all of us.

The April Fabb investigation remains open and even now, April's name resonates in the media and public eye with a force that few would have expected so long after her tragic disappearance.

Ian McPherson MBA, Dip.App.Crim
Chief Constable Norfolk Constabulary
October 2007

Prologue

Write of things thou hast seen, and the things which are, and the things which shall be hereafter. Revelation 1.19

Ju** uly 1997 and a Tornado jet fighter roars low over the North Norfolk countryside, its suddenness, power and noise startling people on the ground. An hour later the aircraft roars back on a reciprocal course, returning after another hour on a bisecting course before winging away, mission accomplished, at the time classified, now, ten years later, to be revealed. Technically advanced equipment had searched where others had looked more primitively twenty-eight years earlier. A modern age sought to answer Norfolk's outstanding question. Where is April Fabb? Time does not admit defeat.

'The Lost Years – The Story of April Fabb' was published in 1995 to give impetus to a then twenty-six years old inquiry and the prologue stated: 'To write of tragedy is, potentially, to inflict pain; to write of mystery is to invite explanation, even solution.' That solution did not arrive in 1995, or after. There is still time.

Over the years requests to reprint 'The Lost Years' have been resisted on the grounds that April's book was not purely a commercial venture. It sought to inform, inspire new information and, through sales, provide a memorial to a lost girl, something for a family to relate to from the emptiness and agony of the unknown. The book sold out in a few weeks and the memorial stands near the door of St Andrew's Church at Metton. Inside the church the visitors' book confirms that April has truly not been forgotten.

The primary objective of 'The Lost Years' was, still is, to find her, and what happened to her. Now, in 2007, in response to renewed requests, and with the support of her family, who have never given up hope, and the Norfolk Constabulary, who have never given up looking for her, 'The Lost Years' appears in a new guise but with the same primary objective. The book is substantially as before but revised, developed and updated and, as before, seeking the greatest development of all – the discovery of April.

The 1995 prologue stated: 'April was a young girl, happy, contented, expecting the fulfilment of adulthood shared with the family that raised her, a future denied in mysterious circumstances, leading to years of speculating agony, a void of lost years that can never be replaced ... She, and the facts of this long ago case should not be forgotten: not while others still pray for the explanation that may yet be delivered.' These words are changeless. The search is unending, the case for a new edition of 'The Lost Years' irresistible.

What follows is more than a new edition re-booting an old investigation; it is another reminder and memorial to a young girl and caring relatives still wrestling with their grief, to the unkindness of life, and the agony of the unknown. If it spurs new information, re-concentrates thoughts dimmed by time and opens new lines of inquiry then so much the better. Gone is not forgotten.

ILLUSTRATIONS

Page

Cover: April Fabb, her abandoned cycle and Back Lane
Frontispiece: April Fabb
1.1	Geography of a mystery. The police plan	17
1.2	St Andrew's Church, Metton	19
1.3	A younger April with her mother, father and sister Diane	21
1.4	April with her much loved dog, Trudy	22
2.1	The police sketch of April's clothing	28
2.2	The beginning of a fateful journey	29
2.3	The last happy place: a field now without a donkey	30
2.4	The last sighting: approaching Pillar Box Corner	31
2.5	First sighting of the abandoned cycle	32
2.6	April Fabb's cycle at Constable Chiddick's house	34
2.7	Back Lane viewed from Pillar Box Corner	36
2.8	Looking towards Pillar Box Corner from a point April did not reach	36
3.1	Reg Lester makes notes as officers assemble	43
3.2	Headlines 9 April 1969	43
3.3	John Dye and Reg Taylor in the Incident Room	45
3.4	Police display April's photograph at Cromer Railway Station	46
4.1	Dick Bass studies the cycle repositioned in Three Corner Field	50
4.2	The repositioned cycle	51
4.3	Reg Lester stands where a kidnapper may have stood	52
4.4	A search team confers in open country	54
4.5	Probing hedgerows	54
4.6	A haystack is dismantled	55
4.7	Police frogmen searching Felbrigg Lake	56
5.1	Reg Lester and Albert Fabb outside 3 Council Houses	63
5.2	An unrealised destination. Back Lane emerges onto the B1436	69
5.3	Vehicle numbers recorded by juvenile spotters	71
6.1	A family waits. Mr and Mrs Fabb with their daughter Pamela and grandson Duncan, April's friend Susan, and April's dog Trudy	78

6.2 A notice on a church door, 1969–1995   80
6.3 A memorial, 1995 onward   80
6.4 Just a part of the public response   83
6.5 An anonymous and regular Easter message to a
     distraught family   84
6.6 An anonymous and cryptic message to a national newspaper 85
7.1 A poignant picture in 1972. Olive Fabb stands at April's
     last known place   92
7.2 Albert and Olive Fabb in St Andrew's Church   93
8.1 Lonely sentinels stand over an unchanging scene.   103
8.2 April's treasured doll's house   107
9.1 Reg Lester sits next to Mr and Mrs Fabb at the 1989
     press conference   114
9.2 1993 and renewed publicity   115
10.1 The last known picture of April, part of the film of a
     school trip   120
10.2 The police file is still open   126
Epilogue: A corner of a churchyard that is forever April's 132

A Notice and a Country Place

The rain lashed Easter of 1994 was unremarkable, except for an anniversary; an anniversary poignantly marked on paper pinned to a church door for a quarter of a century, calling for the attention of all who sought to enter: worshippers, travellers, historians, and a writer. Thirteen years later Easter is blessed with fine weather and the written notice has gone, replaced by a stone memorial by the church door. The anniversary has moved on to thirty-eight years.

Whether by pinned notice or stone memorial, a visit to the attractive fifteenth century church, prominently posed above a hamlet of dwellings, reveals a unique message from the past, history reaching out; compelling history that has absorbed many travellers and church visitors and continues to consume the still living participants of a tale of tragedy. Reading the message turns interest into intrigue. Here is a glimpse of a heartbreaking story, captivating the chance traveller or deliberate visitor, well-known to the people of Norfolk, though fading through the passage of time and succession of those unborn during traumatic times so long ago.

How many traversing the grey sodden landscape of North Norfolk at Easter 1994, battered by flurries of snow and sleet, or the better weather of 2007, would recall the gloriously sunny Easter of 1969? A time when holidaymakers and picnickers were much in evidence, when farmers took advantage of the dryness to till the fields, schoolchildren celebrated the holiday by playing in regular sunshine, and the promise of summer erased the memory of winter; all encompassed in the unspoilt countryside radiating from the coastal resorts of Cromer and Sheringham.

This idyllic perspective was, on one day, within a definition of minutes, but almost certainly seconds, to change for all who were to become aware of an incident in which a young girl was lost, affecting not just family, friends, the people of Norfolk, but noticed nationally. Inexplicable circumstances were retold, examined, re-examined and endured to occupy the attention of so many, including church visitors.

A church visitor may, prompted by book, notice or memorial, learn of the lost years from 1969 onwards; years when much was done but nothing was found; when a child should have grown to a young woman; when a family experienced the heartbreak of what might have been without knowing why it could not be.

The story bound to the notice and memorial often appears in general overview, laced with speculation, opinion, and some infilling guesswork. The facts of history and geography are more detailed and the reader may, using imagination, deduction, perception, intuition, finally arrive at a conclusion, or just an opinion, or perhaps become just another hapless observer of the unexplained, the inconclusive, the tragedy of the known underlined by the agony of the unknown.

The known facts can be described without argument. Explanation, analysis and the ending are more conjectural. In fact, there is no ending. That is the point.

Descriptions of what happened, or may have happened, were supplied at the time, recalled from memories that had not been tuned to abnormality within a normal day. Therefore, inevitably, there is a framework of uncorroborated recollection with inconsistencies of detail within. The power of recall is debatable, dependent upon the prompt, the timescale, the incentive. It follows that at the time of an incident, occurrence or sequence in one's life, perception of the ordinary and routine may be insecure or superficial, and retrospection, even with the help of others, will not always reveal the truth. Much of this case remains unknown. What is known is that tragedy becomes apparent, evil presumed, but mystery predominates.

So begins a journey of understanding, commencing with an appreciation of the handsome geography of North Norfolk. Driving through the attractive countryside it is easy to appreciate the wide, sweeping, rural scenery, the tranquillity and the even pace of unstressed life, the quiet, orderly, almost soporific, environment created by a beautiful sunny day in 1969. But this was a day someone was to indelibly mark into the annals of Norfolk history by action unknown but circumstantially presumed, which still calls for explanation and detail. Was this person a stranger? An intruder? Someone lost or exploring? Travelling a known route? A local person?

Or persons? How did they come to be where they were – in an isolated country lane on a gloriously warm day? An accident of time, place and person, or more sinisterly premeditated? Only by understanding the geography can a view be expressed.

The A140 road connects Cromer with Norwich, some 25 miles apart, and the B1436 road diverts from it at Roughton, going towards the Sheringham coast road, running through Roughton and Felbrigg, passing the fine old mansion of Felbrigg Hall. Those wishing to visit more obscure localities will deviate into side roads, either with knowledge of a destination or, sometimes, lost in the spirit of exploration, or perhaps just lost.

Side roads from the B1436 road are narrow, uninviting to heavy traffic, and used only with local knowledge or by the most venturesome driver. Signposts indicate rarely heard names: Sustead, Gresham, Aylmerton, Metton and Northrepps.

A forked junction, not far from the Felbrigg Hall entrance, offers a variety of destinations but in 2007 names but one, Metton. This road receives its occasional vehicle, mostly from the Cromer direction, with a due lessening of speed in deference to the sudden reduction in available width. For all its narrowness and isolation, it is the principal road from Cromer and Felbrigg into Metton.

Within the view of the Cromer to Metton road there is a higher level converging and even narrower road from Roughton, separated by a field known as, appropriately, Three Corner Field, at the point of which is the dog leg junction with the Cromer road: a place known as Pillar Box Corner, but with the pillar box long gone. This higher narrower road, known as Back Lane, is a local cut-through route that will not permit the passage of opposing normal sized vehicles, though alleviating the problem for its length alongside Three Corner Field by the visibility afforded by its absolute straightness.

Back Lane and Three Corner Field embrace the scene, the place where it, whatever, happened. The exact spot is known: after that, mystery. The place remains relatively unchanged in 2007, the straight asphalted narrow lane still flanked by grassy banks, the same trees towering over the spot – if only they could talk.

2007 visitors will find the overall area almost a time warp from 1969, perhaps a little less picturesque in places – more traffic – though still sporadic, but essentially the same, requiring only the return of the role players of the sixties.

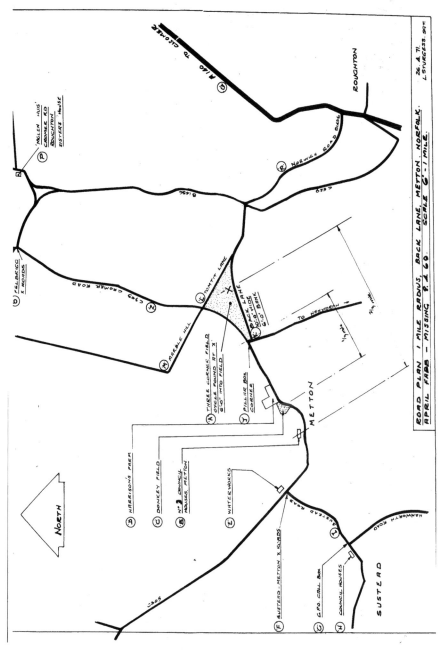

Figure 1.1 Geography of a mystery. The police plan.
Copyright of Norfolk Constabulary

The exploring driver of today probably uses the more prominent route, the Cromer road, driving carefully into the forked junction towards Metton, anxiously scanning ahead for opposing traffic as the narrow road undulates and winds into a valley flanked by grassy banks and overlooked by rolling fields in an attention seeking vista that threatens the driver's concentration. On the left, on a higher plane, the roof of a moving vehicle will reveal the presence of Back Lane.

After the joining of the Cromer road and Back Lane at Pillar Box Corner, Hall Farm is passed on the right, next a grassed field that was of importance in 1969 when it contained a donkey; now it is empty.

Now the road requires absolute concentration as it twists and turns into a series of blind bends, hills and dips of unimproving width accentuated by an absent footpath and the proximity of an assorted collection of houses and cottages, all dominated by the overseeing flint church sitting prominently on the left.

Breasting the crest of the hill, past the church, a downhill curve releases the driver into a straight stretch of road. The few habitats have gone; more open unpopulated countryside lies ahead. A signpost advises Sustead via the minor road on the left, or Gresham straight on, and points back to Metton, a hamlet of some fifty souls; on a fine day almost entrancing in its chocolate box beauty, awkward to navigate but unspoilt and timeless – a place without shops, public house, community hall or other representation of modern life, a place passed in seconds with utmost concentration, a place worth another look.

The driver has choices. Straight on for Gresham, an improved, reasonable looking road, or left for more of the narrow and unknown, the small village of Sustead, eventually on through a tortuous route to the market town of Aylsham. Or back to Metton!

Does the driver realise the historical significance of Metton? Does the name jar a chord? Perhaps there was a reason to stop and discover that this was no ordinary rural retreat. Many have searched for the tiny hamlet, and motives have been various, mostly researching and investigating, dwelling upon the atmosphere, marvelling at the incongruity of peace with mystery, intrigue with normality.

The locale is attractive, best appreciated without the concentration of a vehicle; the driver returns up the hill and parks in the most obvious place, alongside the church, opposite a row of houses that are decorative in appearance but more subdued by name. They are known simply as 'Council Houses'.

St Andrew's Church, splendid and dominant, cries out as a starting and a viewing point; it is from here the unsuspecting visitor first realises that Metton is a place of significance, a scene of tragedy, a place of mystery that never ceases to torture and agonise, and a place of homage and reverence: for our pre-1995 visitor it is displayed on the church door, bold calligraphic writing protected by cellophane. The notice reads:

> *'Will you of your charity remember in your prayers April Fabb, a child who disappeared from this parish in April 1969 – of whom nothing has since been heard. Please remember also the parents & relatives who still wait & hope.'*

If our visitor has arrived in the later years, when the notice has given birth to a permanent memorial, a similar message is carved in stone above fresh flowers.

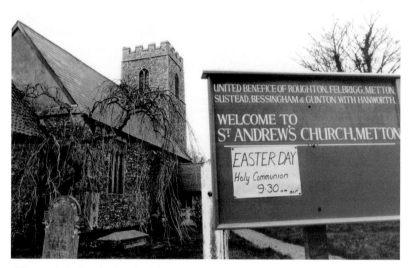

Figure 1.2 St Andrew's Church. Mystery and tragedy are recorded here

The visitor, moving from the tragic message to the grassed frontage of the church, wonders about the happenings of 1969 and, using the lofty vantage point, surveys the area of the disappearance, from the Council Houses immediately opposite to the winding road and fields dwindling into the distance. How could a child disappear from such a restful, untouched area? What circumstances could possibly have surrounded such an event in such a place?

The Council Houses are a permanent reminder of the start of April Fabb's last journey; number 3 was her home, her birth place, the beginning of the end. Her house faces the church. From the nearby churchyard the thoughtful visitor may look into the distance, across fields to a small line of roadside trees in Back Lane: the end of April's journey - and all knowledge from then on.

The question posed by many, whether they are visitors reflecting in a grassy churchyard, empathetic outsiders or inquiring investigators - and there have been great numbers of each, is: who was April Fabb? What kind of child could have been so unfortunate as to disappear from the face of the earth without visible trace, from a rural retreat that promised quality of life and was rarely bothered by crime or outsiders? The answer can only deepen the mystery, heighten the tragedy.

April Fabb may have been described as a child but she was approaching young womanhood, a blue eyed, fair haired, well developed young girl with a pretty oval face. Her pleasantly shy manner was appropriate to a young country girl intent upon her own interests, displaying a naturally quiet companionship and a diffidence to strangers, traits that would later occupy the minds of many who had never met her.

She would have been fourteen years of age on 22 April 1969. That she never reached that birthday with her family is an enduring mystery that has troubled and exercised the minds of a vast number of persons to whom the name is now commonplace, associated automatically with the inexplicable, almost a *Mary Celeste* circumstance to live on into eternity.

At Easter 1969 she was a normal happy girl with a settled, contented family life, the youngest of three girls and one of two still living at home with her parents, an unassuming couple devoted to each other and their three daughters. Her father, Albert Ernest Fabb, called Albert by some, Ernest by others (so addressed by the police and press), inexplicably 'Jack' by his workmates, but always Albert to his wife, was a sociable, hard working and well respected man. He worked as a builder's labourer in Cromer.

April's mother, Olive Fabb, a homely, pleasant and caring woman, worked part time at the church rectory. Sister Diane, aged twenty-one years, worked in Cromer as a clerk in a furniture store.

The eldest sister, Pamela, was twenty-seven years of age. She was married and lived in Roughton with her husband Bernard and baby Duncan, just over a mile away: in fact just a cycle ride away. The three sisters were close to each other in affection as well as geography.

April's life revolved around Metton, Cromer, and to some extent the surrounding villages. She attended Cromer Secondary Modern School where she had several friends, shared with those formed within her own area of Metton. Her love of the countryside was entwined with her home life and there was little temptation to go further afield.

Sometimes she accompanied her parents on shopping trips to Norwich, but she did not share her father's keen interest in Norwich City Football Club. Bingo was more enjoyable and she looked forward to visits to the nearby village of Aylmerton with her elder sister's father-in-law, playing the game in the local hall. The bingo sessions finished at Christmas but not before April had notched up wins of 12/6d, 10/- and £1. This money she placed in a jar in her bedroom. She was a careful girl who knew the value of money.

Pocket money of 4/- a week was converted into savings stamps and a Post Office Savings book recorded a small amount regularly saved.

Figure 1.3 A younger April (right), with her mother,
father and sister Diane

She was interested in animals with a particular fondness for cats, several of whom appeared at her home, either voluntarily or by her instigation, where she groomed and paid detailed attention to their paws. Every cat left April with clean paws.

The resident pet was a dog. April's lovable and excitable cairn terrier, Trudy, occupied much of her mistress's time with walks and play and April was extremely fond of the little terrier that her been her close companion for the past three years.

Figure 1.4 April with her much loved dog, Trudy

Hobbies of stamp collecting and needlework also occupied April's time, indeed, she was accomplished at dressmaking and embroidery, taking great pride in making her own clothes, though sometimes susceptible to the feminine change of mind, evidenced by Diane finding her poised with scissors about to cut up a dress that no longer gave satisfaction. A swift claim halted the scissors and Diane became the owner of a new dress made by her younger sister.

Although shy in manner April did meet the general public when she obtained seasonal work helping in a tea shop at Cromer, serving teas, ice cream and other light refreshments, earning 10/- a day. She also occasionally baby sat for farmer Harrison at Hall Farm in Metton with her friend Susan, earning 2/6d an hour.

Very occasionally, April would go with her friends, Susan, who lived in Metton, and Gillian, who lived in Northrepps, to the cinema at Cromer, and even more rarely she attended school dances or a dance at East Runton Village Hall.

Boy friends had yet to impress her but she was keenly interested in certain pop singers and groups. Top of the Pops was her favourite television programme (viewed in black and white), and the lead singer of the group Amen Corner, Andy Fairweather Lowe, was her special favourite: he was later to send her an invitation, when her name was on every tongue and she was unable to respond.

Altogether April was a normal, quiet country girl leading a contented, happy life with her family in an environment that she knew well and loved. Her life had not experienced too much change or reached new horizons for she was born and raised in the house in which she lived – and was to disappear from.

In March 1969, April announced that she needed some material to make a summer dress at school. She asked if she could accompany her friend Susan to Norwich at Easter to purchase the material and her mother agreed. The girls were to cycle to Roughton, leave their cycles at Pamela's home, and catch the bus to Norwich: an exciting prospect for two young girls. It was arranged for the Wednesday after Easter [9 April]. Mrs Fabb made the prospect more pleasurable by agreeing to pay for the material.

In the prelude to Easter, April rode over to Roughton, via Back Lane, to a sweet shop. There she purchased chocolates as a present for her brother-in-law, Bernard: it was his birthday on Easter Monday. Unfortunately, or fortunately, April also liked chocolates and they did not survive beyond Easter Saturday. Originally they were placed in her doll's house in her room but temptation removed them.

The school holiday began on 28 March, the Friday before Good Friday, and the school coach dropped April at her front door at the usual time of four pm. Two weeks of leisure, time to pursue individual interests, lay ahead. And on the Wednesday after Easter there was the much anticipated trip to Norwich.

The holiday did not start well. April spent the Saturday and Sunday in bed with a sore throat, also much of the Monday. Tuesday was a better day, the first day of the month of April. She took Trudy for a walk and later accompanied her mother to Cromer on the bus. This was an enjoyable visit because her mother bought her a pair of new shoes. April, feeling better, walked to her sister Pamela's bungalow at Roughton.

Later in the afternoon, Mrs Fabb, walking to Pamela's home, came upon April pushing the pram containing Pamela's baby, April's nephew Duncan, a volunteered task made more enjoyable by the fine weather. After returning home on the bus April obtained yet more exercise by again walking Trudy. The busy day continued. During the evening she walked to Hall Farm to show her new shoes to her friend Susan who was babysitting for the Harrisons.

The next day, Wednesday, was also pleasantly spent; walking Pamela's baby, visiting Hall Farm and friends, watching evening television.

On Thursday, April cycled to Northrepps to see her friend Gillian, joining her mother at Pamela's home later that day. She accepted a lift from the visiting father-in-law of Pamela and returned home in his car with her cycle in the boot; her mother returned later. That evening April and Susan took Trudy for a walk and returned with the little terrier covered in mud, an event that brought despairing comment from April's mother.

The holiday had so far been interesting and satisfying, enhanced by the fine weather which allowed April the regular use of her cycle, a smart blue and white BSA Star Rover model with white saddle and saddle bag, a cycle that she was outgrowing. (Her father had been thinking of a replacement).

On Good Friday, April and Diane cycled together to see Gillian at Northrepps and from there Diane went on to see her boyfriend. April met some of her school friends and also Gillian's holidaying boyfriend who had a car. He volunteered to take them all to the beach. The afternoon was consequently spent at Overstrand beach, although April and her friend Jane made only a brief inspection of the sea before retiring to buy sweets in a nearby shop. Time was then spent leaning on railings watching the others cavorting on the sand. April seemed in a pensive mood and, with Jane, decided to walk back towards home. They did not go far because Jane's aunt stopped in her car and gave them a lift to Northrepps.

Saturday was engaged with dog walking, flower gathering, visiting Hall Farm and, in the evening, with her mother, visiting Pamela.

April and Susan decorated the church with wild flowers they had picked, but some primroses were reserved for number 3 Council Houses. The weather continued warm and sunny.

Easter Sunday saw the Fabb family meeting at Pamela and Bernard's home at Roughton. This was a regular get together for a meal and represented the closeness of the family. It was the last time they were to be together.

April and Susan had visited Pamela in the morning, returning home at midday, April later going out without her cycle to be found at Pamela's bungalow when her mother visited in the afternoon. April had walked to Roughton. Later, her father and Diane arrived for the complete family meal. All was well until April got fed-up with the choice of television programmes and walked home, an unusual move because the light was fading and she was frightened of the dark. When her family returned she was watching the programme of her choice.

Easter Monday was a home loving day for April, a beautiful day with unrestrained sunshine enhancing the rural peacefulness, new green leaves and blossoming trees signalling a change to a more clothed, decorated countryside in which the quietness was penetrated only by singing birds and the occasional hum of a passing vehicle. Both she and Diane declined an invitation to accompany their parents to view the ancient ruins at Baconsthorpe. April declared a distinct lack of interest in old ruins. She preferred to enjoy the continuing fine weather in home surrounds with her dog, a decision much appreciated by the little cairn terrier. Diane stayed at home in the morning but then cycled to Cromer to see her boyfriend. April was left, sprawled on the lawn with her friend Christine (Susan's sister), reading books. It was a happy day spent with family, friends and a small dog. It was the last.

Upon the return of her parents April asked, 'Have you got the handkerchief that you are keeping for Bernard's birthday present?'

Her mother said she had the handkerchief and April explained she had arranged for Susan to bring a present from Cromer that she, April, could give to Bernard. She would give both presents at the same time. Her mother presumed this would be the next day and handed over the handkerchief. April left it on the living room mantelpiece. Tomorrow was another day, promising to be as unhurried, peaceful, and as happy as today.

The church visitor would know nothing of the happiness of the last hours of this young girl so many years earlier. There was only the church notice or memorial, each a proclamation, call of distress and plea for all right minded persons to sympathise, grieve and wonder. The message, written or carved in stone, does not mark the detail or the place; it does not relieve the perplexity of an observer attempting to come to terms with a widely viewed area containing the incomprehensible. The declaration reaches out to create amazement and sorrow, and bewilderment caused by an attempt to reconcile the place with the message.

Some detail is known, recorded for posterity to ponder upon: the spot where it, whatever, happened, and when, and the places of preceding action. Tuesday, 8 April 1969 was the day the world stopped for the Fabb family.

A Farewell and a Cycle Ride

A warm sun streaming across a hushed landscape created a hypnotic, soothing atmosphere in the after lunch, early afternoon period of the day after Easter Monday 1969. It seemed a hint or promise of better times ahead and the good weather was conducive to feelings of well-being, enjoyed by people doing different things, shortly to be bound by a common theme.

David Empson, a thirty-four years old man from Sustead, had taken his mother to Cromer Hospital and was using the waiting time to walk his young son among the town's shops. He would before long begin his journey home, taking his mother to Gresham via Felbrigg, going through Metton on the Cromer road: a journey that was to have far reaching consequences and be engraved upon his memory until his death.

Other traffic would soon be heading towards Metton: a Land Rover from the Felbrigg direction, a van with three surveyors from the Gresham direction. Persons in Metton would be moving out: a man going to work at Roughton, farmer Harrison leaving Hall Farm to obtain new machine parts at North Walsham. Others remained in Metton: the tractor driver quietly chugging along the field next to the farm, workers toiling in the field, the man and his wife with four dogs picnicking in Tom Tit Lane - a track that bordered Three Corner Field and connected the Cromer road and Back Lane. Two girls played with a donkey in the grassed field next to the farm, soon to greet, gossip with, and say goodbye to a third girl who would cycle away along the Cromer road towards Pillar Box Corner. This girl was April Fabb, seen again, almost certainly, by the Land Rover driver and by the person or persons with all the answers.

April's day had started slowly with a lie-in, possibly contemplating the uncommitted time ahead, the relaxing, casual euphoria of knowing that the holiday stretched through the week while others returned to the routine of work. Her father left for work at seven-thirty, her sister Diane at five-past-eight. It was another sunny day, promising to be gloriously warm by the afternoon. It boded well for the shopping trip to Norwich the following day.

April was excited and looking forward to her visit to Norwich, when she would be able to browse through material for the summer dress she was going to make. But today would be made up as she went along. There were no problems, no pressing engagements, just a day to be savoured in fine sunshine with time to walk, play or cycle. Perhaps she thought of a visit to her elder sister; a day late for her brother-in-law's birthday and with the intended present gone, though easily replaced, it was a logical contender for some part of the day, especially with weather that invited open air activity: a cycle ride for instance.

Olive Fabb had seen her husband and daughter Diane off to work and, with April still in bed, she walked over to the rectory at nine-thirty. She returned at ten-fifteen to collect some dusters and found April was in the act of getting up, unhurried and unfussed, undecided upon her day's programme. Mrs Fabb returned to the rectory.

Mrs Fabb returned home at about twelve-fifteen to find an empty house. April was out with her dog but she returned within a few minutes of her mother's return. Shortly afterwards there was disappointment when Susan's mother arrived with a note written by Susan explaining that the planned trip to Norwich was off. Susan was employed during the school holidays at a Cromer hotel and was unable to get time off from her job.

Never a demonstrative girl, April was, nevertheless, very disappointed and the odd tear marked this change in her fortunes. Susan's mother commiserated but also, fatefully, handed over ten Player's Weights cigarettes, the present obtained by Susan for April to give to Bernard; a visit by April to her brother-in-law was now very much in focus. Questioned by her mother, April said she had changed her mind about buying chocolates.

April was thoughtful over dinner with her mother, which she concluded at one-thirty with the announcement she was going to telephone her friend Gillian (presumably from the telephone kiosk at Sustead because there was no public telephone in Metton) to ask her if she would go with her to Norwich on Wednesday, the very next day. She quickly left the house, certainly taking her cycle for she was back within ten minutes. The news was good. April told her mother that Gillian would go with her to Norwich on Saturday.

A happier April made another decision. While helping her mother to wash up she said she would take the cigarettes to Bernard, adding that she did not have anything to do that afternoon. She went upstairs to change her clothes.

Originally wearing a green jumper and brown slacks, April reappeared with the same jumper but a wine coloured woollen skirt, long white socks and wooden soled sandals with red straps and brass buckles. She had brushed and swept her hair back into a bunch, tied with a brown crinkly ribbon.

Her mother was not surprised at the change from the slacks for they were in poor condition and she would have insisted on her daughter changing them before visiting her sister. She did, however, note with a little surprise the long white socks: they were not one of April's favourite modes of dress. A touch of lipstick was apparent, but this was usual when April visited her sister.

Figure 2.1 The police sketch of April's clothing.
Copyright of Norfolk Constabulary

April asked her mother for birthday wrapping paper but there was none. A paper bag was obtained from the pantry.

The handkerchief was retrieved from the mantelpiece and April placed the cigarettes inside the folds before placing the composite package in the paper bag.

As April prepared to leave she picked up fivepence-halfpenny she had left on the table. She spoke to her mother for the last time.

'Are you coming with me, mum?'

Her mother replied, 'No, I'm going to do some sewing.'

'Do you think I shall need a coat?' April asked.

'I can't think so,' her mother responded, 'it's so warm.'

'Cheerio,' called April and, with this final farewell, she left the house.

Her mother, watching from the

window, saw April collect her cycle from the garage and ride down the drive to the front gate, turning left into the road and out of sight. The time was between two pm and ten-past-two.

Olive Fabb turned to her household duties with a simple everyday memory of a daughter leaving on a cycle, a memory that would normally erase itself with the passage of time and the return of the daughter. This was to be different. The view from the window would remain unchanged but the girl would not appear within it again. The recall of the last time was to be cemented in the mind of the mother for all time.

April had not declared the route of her journey, but only two alternatives to Roughton existed. Normally, the road from Metton to Felbrigg (the Cromer road) to the forked junction with the B1436, then turning right into the Roughton road. Straightforward, open, and while not exactly a wide road, offering more room than the alternative Back Lane, which reached the B1436 necessitating a left turn into the Roughton road. Events were to show that it was, fatefully, Back Lane.

Why should Back Lane be favoured? One answer was simple: the Roughton sweet shop lay on the route, almost at the junction with the B1436. April liked sweets and was in possession of some money. This was the logical route if the shop was to be visited, but it was also a reasonable route to Pamela's home and had been used before.

Figure 2.2 Strong spring sunshine replicates the beginning of a fateful journey: photographed from St Andrew's churchyard. The road sweeps downhill from the Council Houses to the donkey field

April's journey was quickly broken, a little over a hundred yards from her home, when she came upon a counter attraction, especially to the animal loving country girl; the farmer's donkey, kept in the field next to the road and available to the local children with the farmer's permission, was being ridden by April's friends.

Figure 2.3 The last happy place: a field now without a donkey

The grassed field bordered both road and farm and was on April's left as she cycled downhill from her home. Enjoying themselves in the bright sunshine were Christine, the ten years old younger sister of Susan, and twelve years old Maureen, both playing and riding the amiable donkey back and forth, or trying to, for the animal was exhibiting some of the stubborn traits for which the breed is famous.

Christine called 'Hello' and April shouted back before stopping and propping her cycle at the gate. She entered the field. The three girls spent the next few minutes pleasantly chatting, leading, riding, pushing and stroking the donkey; but it was only a brief sojourn for a decision had been made and April felt compelled to continue her journey. She explained that she was visiting her sister and, bidding her friends goodbye, she remounted her cycle. They watched her cycle away past the farm.

Christine and Maureen estimated that April stayed with them for about ten minutes, having arrived just after two pm. The time of her departure was, therefore, between two-ten and two-fifteen. How precise this estimation may be is subject to individual recollections but it is opened slightly by the Land Rover driver travelling towards Metton from Felbrigg, approaching Hall Farm along the Cromer road. His journey start time was known to be two o'clock and a later re-run of his trip placed him on the road approaching the farm and the donkey field at six minutes past two, at the very place where he saw a young girl riding a blue and white cycle on the wrong side of the road, not far from, and obviously preparatory to turning right at Pillar Box Corner and the dog leg junction into Back Lane.

That the Land Rover driver saw April Fabb there can be no doubt. He was the last identified person to do so. But others were very close to seeing her a few minutes later.

At a finely judged time of two-fifteen, three surveyors were approaching Pillar Box Corner in their van, travelling through Metton from Gresham, when their attention was drawn to a cycle lying in the field separating the Cromer road and Back Lane. The cycle was lying a few feet from the bank on the Back Lane side of the field, some distance away from them but clearly visible. They noted this strange circumstance with breaking their journey. Later they were to be aware of an awful significance, while others were to ponder upon the relevance of the cycle's position at that time. Had its rider, and someone else, been on the other side of the bank, in Back Lane, at the very time the cycle was first spotted?

Figure 2.4 The last sighting: approaching Pillar Box Corner.
April's cycle was found top right (circled)

Figure 2.5 First sighting of the abandoned cycle, seen from the Cromer
road: a scene reconstructed and photographed by the police.
Copyright of Norfolk Constabulary

Whether April, and others, were present when the cycle was first
seen in the field is conjectural, but what is known, without doubt, is
the unconscious presence of persons within a short distance of
whatever took place: persons who sought to enjoy the early afternoon
sunshine without thought of drama or crisis, but whose nearness
could have been influential if called upon.

From one pm until just after three pm, within a few hundred yards
of whatever happened, an elderly couple from Sustead reclined in
small chairs with their four dogs running loose. Relaxing in the
aftermath of an enjoyable picnic they drank in the balmy, undisturbed
atmosphere, oblivious of anything other than the peace that
surrounded them. They, and their car, were screened in Tom Tit Lane
and they neither heard nor saw anything, though this may be related
to them dozing between one-forty and two-fifty pm. They were,
however, adamant that their dogs would have barked at any
disturbance. This amazing coincidence of proximity in a rural
landscape yielded not one positive lead to those who were later to
grapple with the inexplicable.

Conclusions that may be drawn from the negative are discussed
later. What is incontrovertible is the time factor that indisputably put

people nearby at the most dramatic time of all. How close was salvation, if April had known.

Such a relevance of time was not applicable to David Empson driving his Vauxhall Viva along the Cromer road towards Metton. It was about three pm and his mother, looking from the nearside passenger seat, saw the cycle lying in the field. She pointed it out to her son who reacted by turning left at Pillar Box Corner to enter Back Lane, from where the cycle could not be seen. It was hidden by the roadside bank. Stopping at the estimated point, Empson climbed the bank, entered the field, and inspected what he viewed as a perfectly good cycle incongruously lying several feet into a ploughed field. After discussing the phenomenon with his mother he placed the cycle in his car and drove to the police house at Roughton, only a few minutes away, a move he was later to publicly regret.

Police Constable Chiddick was a county police officer used to sharing his home with the vagaries and responsibilities of a regular police station, something that came as second nature to county police officers but was less usual, and not altogether welcome, to their city brethren. He was at home when David Empson arrived with a smart looking cycle found in a ploughed field: unusual and further complicated when he looked in the saddlebag for some clue as to the owner. He discovered a paper bag which in turn revealed a handkerchief, fivepence-halfpenny and ten Player's Weights cigarettes.

The constable listened carefully to Empson's description of his find, which included the opinion that the cycle was possibly stolen. The officer refrained from opinion but was not disposed to disagree with this early view, little knowing that he was to be the first of a long line of police officers seeking an answer to the circumstances that placed this cycle in a field.

After noting the details, Constable Chiddick placed the cycle in his garage, thanked and dismissed the finder, and informed his police station at Cromer. Later he was to be on duty at Cromer Police Station when the owner of the cycle would become apparent along with the dreadful significance of its abandonment. At that time his knowledge of what had happened could only have been speculative, based on a paucity of fact. That position has changed little over thirty-eight years.

*Figure 2.6 April Fabb's cycle at Constable Chiddick's house;
a police 'scenes of crime' van is in the background.*

Copyright of Norfolk Constabulary

Lengthening shadows and a lowering sun moved afternoon into evening as Metton quietly slipped towards the end of another day. Mrs Fabb busied herself at home and awaited the return of her family, not unduly concerned when only her husband and daughter Diane presented themselves for the evening meal. Her immediate thought was that April was staying at her sisters for something to eat, engaged in an interesting and time consuming visit. Without private telephones it was something that could not be checked, but as time passed and the light began to fail twinges of anxiety gave way to serious concern. April was a considerate girl and would not unduly alarm her parents. Neither would she cycle home in the dark: one reason was that her cycle did not have lights, but more importantly she was frightened of the dark. Something was not right. Mrs Fabb collected her own cycle and made haste to her daughter Pamela's address at Roughton. The time was eight forty-five.

There followed the most dreadful moment of Olive Fabb's life. Her anxious question, seeking relief and confirmation of April's well-being, received an innocent, quizzical answer from her other daughter, which precipitated the heart stopping realisation that something terrible had happened.

Pamela's statement that April had not been seen that day turned alarm into pronounced fear, a fear that agonised a mother and instigated immediate, frantic, desperately hopeful enquiries that prayed for, but could not see, a quick, happy and natural explanation.

Bernard, Pamela's husband, telephoned Gillian at Sustead; April had not been seen. More, urgent, enquiries followed.

Cycling towards her home in a state of desperate apprehension Olive Fabb met her husband walking the dog. She gasped the awful news. A quick verifying check at 3 Council Houses did not reveal April. An alarmed Diane raced to sisters' Susan and Christine's home: to no avail. April had not been seen since leaving the donkey in the field. Diane and her father immediately went to the rectory where the vicar telephoned Cromer Hospital. The hospital had no knowledge of April or anyone like her. The vicar telephoned Cromer police.

Shock and terror can come in different forms, from many sources, but the Fabb family were experiencing the rapid build-up of the most awful adrenalin draining sensation of impending disaster, reinforced by the absence of news in any form. Calling the police was the final act that forced acceptance that a perfectly natural explanation was not just around the corner; they were not about to be reunited, laughing with relief at the sudden happy ending. Above all, it was the realisation that something had already almost certainly happened, and time was slipping away. That time was to slip away for the next thirty-eight years.

At ten o'clock that night Constable Chiddick answered the telephone at Cromer Police Station. A man wished to report a missing girl, nearly fourteen years of age and not been seen since she set out to cycle from Metton to Roughton in the early afternoon. The constable knew that he had discovered the owner of the cycle that now rested in his garage. So began the police investigation into the disappearance of April Fabb.

Missing person reports are not altogether rare in the variety of incidents, events and episodes that appear under the umbrella description of police work. How they are treated depends greatly on the primary evaluation of the person missing, person reporting, and the attendant facts. The telephoned report of April Fabb's disappearance went immediately to the top of the scale of urgency, sinister connotations cried out for an incisive response. Constable Chiddick contacted his section sergeant and apprised him not only of

Figure 2.7 Back Lane viewed from Pillar Box Corner:
photographed by the police.
Copyright of Norfolk Constabulary

Figure 2.8 Back Lane looking towards Pillar Box Corner:
photographed by the police from a point April did not reach.
Copyright of Norfolk Constabulary

the missing person report, but the alarming discovery of a cycle that obviously belonged to the missing girl.

Sergeant Francis was no less apprehensive. He quickly organised visits to friends and relatives that confirmed the absence of April, at the same time informing his divisional headquarters at North Walsham and force headquarters at Norwich.

Detectives joined uniformed officers, interviewing the Fabb family and visiting Back Lane. A search of the road, and adjoining banks and fields, was conducted by torchlight then suspended to wait for morning light.

Mr and Mrs Fabb remained in their home in a restless torment of anticipatory grief that repelled any form of relaxing sleep. Wild primroses in the house marked the recent presence of April; beautiful in appearance yet agonising in their reminder, they were a tangible symbol of happiness so recently evident, now so abruptly shattered. Surely, before they wilted some news would be forthcoming.

A light burned throughout the night, and the door remained unlocked in number 3 Council Houses: but its youngest occupant was not coming back.

Viewed in a Very, Very Serious Light

In the early hours of Wednesday, 9 April, with the first streaks of light glancing across the sky, a telephone rang in a bedroom near Norwich and a sleep ridden voice answered. Reg Lester was not unused to taking out of hours' calls, it was part of his job, but at that at that time of the morning a call was a portent of something serious and urgent. He listened with growing apprehension as the detached voice from police headquarters advised him of a missing person that was a probable abduction, possible murder. It seemed no other interpretation was possible. He dressed and headed for Cromer.

As head of Norfolk CID, Detective Chief Superintendent Lester would automatically take command of an unsolved murder enquiry, reporting directly to the chief constable. He would override the territorial responsibility of the chief superintendent in charge of the police division in which the body had been found, calling upon him to supply manpower for searches, house to house enquiries and other labour intensive tasks, advising him of progress – the policy of which was for the CID to decide. Everyone knew where they stood, where responsibility lay. All media interest was channelled through the man in charge, all enquiries, statements, problems, decisions.

This procedure had a provincial fail-safe, applied by police forces inexperienced in dealing with major crimes that required intensive organisation and expertise: call in Scotland Yard, a phrase much loved and abused by thriller writers, one that needs some practical clarification.

The C Department of New Scotland Yard was comprised of specialist sections designed to deal with special problems, and C1 dealt with major crime, which meant, principally, murders, hence the title applied by journalists – Murder Squad. Dealing with the crime of the nation's capital the department was, naturally, very busy, therefore, experienced and, by necessity, well trained in a systematic approach to murder investigation.

The Metropolitan Police in the form of New Scotland Yard recognised that small police forces with limited resources and experience, especially the latter, could be severely stretched by a difficult major crime investigation. C1 expert assistance was, therefore, made available to the provinces: if requested by the chief constable. The proviso was that the request should be made within the first twenty-four hours of the discovery of the body or instigation of the investigation, not after the local force had kicked over the traces and decided the investigation was a shade too difficult. It was also necessary to have clear evidence that a major crime existed, usually a murder, the best evidence of which was the discovery of a body.

Was April Fabb dead? No one could be sure. Yet the head of CID was hastening to the scene. Not usual for a missing person enquiry. An early decision would be necessary if New Scotland Yard were to be involved; but was outside assistance really necessary when the Norfolk Joint Police was a newly formed emerging force with the ability to carry out the investigation? That was a view that owed something to the confidence and construction of the new force, and something to the absence of the usual prerequisite for the attendance of New Scotland Yard detectives: a body.

How was Norfolk a new force? The word 'new' is artificial in this sense. The force was fifteen months into a new composition when April disappeared, unchanged in content but new in structure and collaboration.

On 1 January 1968, the forces of Great Yarmouth Borough, Norwich City and Norfolk County amalgamated to form the new Norfolk Joint Police, in later years to be renamed Norfolk Constabulary, as it is known today. This new and large single force created bigger departments and higher ranks; it also created a measure of antipathy between some diehards who wished to remain as Great Yarmouth Borough, Norwich City and Norfolk County.

The government induced amalgamation had created size and, presumably, flexibility, power and resources. April Fabb would test the theory as it brought together representatives of all three forces now working under one title, united in a common objective irrespective of previous experience in borough, city or county.

The theory of amalgamation was excellent, but practice would be another matter. Not everyone held the view that the co-ordinated one force was better than three separate forces. Some viewed the new structure as cumbersome and more detached from the public, though they would have found it difficult to argue against the practicality and potential of one united force now facing its severest test. How the Norfolk county force in it its original form would have coped is a theoretical argument that would have attracted partisan views from original loyalties.

The police faced the daunting task of searching a vast rolling countryside, itself a logistical and organisational problem, with the expected outcome of a murder that would entail expert analysis and prioritisation of enquiries, using detectives who would be tackling the most sensational and difficult investigation to have visited any of the three constituent forces within memory. There was a sense of foreboding, combined with a realisation that policing the pleasant and basically law-abiding county of Norfolk had moved on rather ominously. (It was to move on even more ominously with murders and another missing child enquiry in this same year).

These were pioneer and transitional days as provincial police forces availed themselves of training courses at New Scotland Yard and moved towards a new era of self-sufficiency in a systematic, resourceful response to the demands of major investigations. In 1969 the novelists beloved 'call in Scotland Yard' was not so predominant as in previous years, and within a few years all police forces would be weaned off this traditional, almost automatic cry for assistance; not before time in the view of some provincial detectives who found the hard nosed systematic approach of London detectives counter productive in rural localities, where local knowledge usually gained the first foothold.

The sum of the parts was that the new Norfolk force could cope: and without a body might have to. History should not argue with that decision. Yet the Norfolk force had previously called in Scotland Yard and was to again: twice later in 1969 for murders, again in 1970 and again in 1976, these latter cases each being the murder of a young girl, albeit in the 1976 case local detectives had solved the case before the Scotland Yard detectives arrived.

Scotland Yard's attendance was usually in the form of a detective chief superintendent or detective superintendent, with accompanying detective inspector, or maybe detective sergeant. They would apply organisational procedures for receiving, recording, assessing and comparing information; they would prioritise and recommend courses of action consistent with the information received, and they would work alongside the head of CID of the force concerned. The head of Norfolk CID was now heading for Cromer with a view to setting up such procedures.

If April had been found murdered would New Scotland Yard have been called in? The question is hypothetical, the answer seemingly evident.

Above all else there was the question of whether April's disappearance was a serious crime. Very likely, though not everyone thought so; some considered it was very early in the case and perhaps a simple explanation lay just around the corner; others hoped for a happy ending knowing deep down that it was extremely unlikely.

What of the man now charged with finding April? Reg Lester had arrived from Walsall in 1965 to take up the newly created post of detective chief inspector in the Norwich City Police, later transferring to the county force as detective superintendent and, with amalgamation, taking over the CID of the newly joined forces as its first detective chief superintendent. He arrived at Cromer on 9 April 1969 facing a severe, foreboding task.

In police parlance, April Fabb was a missing person and to this day she does not appear in crime statistics, thereby joining the views of her mother, who in the absence of knowledge nurtured hope, and the police who applied the Home Office criteria for recording crime, namely, some evidence of its occurrence. The disappearance was not sufficient. Most people will have difficulty with this assessment in April's case.

The absence of a recorded crime also meant the chief superintendent of the North Walsham Division, within which Cromer lay, had the primary responsibility for maintaining a missing person file with consequent enquiries. That the CID did take charge is a pointer to what was indicated, and expected. The seriousness and implication was obvious, with only a few dissenting voices.

The weather on 9 April deteriorated, becoming cloudy and less warm, further worsening as the week went on, providing a sombre but suitable backcloth to the depressing events occupying the time of a large number of persons. The first action was the daylight search of Back Lane and surrounding fields, hastily organised by officers from Cromer Police Station who initially abandoned a systematic approach for a possible quick result. This and re-interviewing the Fabb family only confirmed the overwhelming mystery and terrible conclusion that April had not been the author of her going.

That the Norfolk Joint Police recognised the gravity of the situation at the outset there can be no doubt. The 'she'll turn up' brigade was minute and muted, more hopeful in expression than convinced by inner feelings. That the most senior detectives in the force were present at the scene within twenty-four hours removes any suggestion that the police commenced a tentative probe designed solely to trace a missing person. Senior detectives feared the worst and the lack of a result from the initial search did nothing to allay their fears.

Reg Lester spoke to Olive and Albert Fabb as both policeman and father. He was to speak to them many times over many years, as policeman, ex-policeman and friend, forming an emotive bond that should not be part of practical police work yet can be admired for its evidence of concern and demonstration of humanity. He was a solemn faced, studiously courteous, impeccably dressed man whose high-pitched Midlands accented voice contrasted noticeably with the broad Norfolk tones that regularly conversed with him. A genuine, intense and sensitive man, he was receptive to the agony of the parents.

An Incident Room was briefly set up at Roughton Village Hall but quickly transferred to Cromer Police Station. The chief constable declared the investigation a 'Special Occasion', which in police terms meant that paid overtime was sanctioned and officers were to be seconded from other duties, and not just from within the North Walsham Division which held geographical jurisdiction. Experienced, qualified and specialist officers were being called in on 9 April. The re-interviews and daylight search had failed. April had gone and there was no trace, no pointer to her whereabouts. More searching, more enquiries; it had to be intensive, organised; it had to be accelerated.

Olive and Albert Fabb sat at home numbly answering police questions, sitting in shocked unbelieving silence as relatives, friends, the vicar, spoke in comforting optimistic tones, vainly attempting to dilute the awful feeling of expectancy that the next caller would bring the worst news of all. A doctor called with a sedative. These two

*Figure 3.1 Reg Lester (centre) stands in front of his car
and makes notes as officers assemble.* Archant (Norfolk)

Figure 3.2 Headlines 9 April 1969 Archant (Norfolk)

honest and extremely pleasant people acknowledged the ministrations of others with massive forbearance and politeness, but Olive Fabb was later to admit that she hated the policeman who asked for a description of the underwear that April was wearing. It was not the man; it was the question he had to ask. The significance was too much.

Other detectives arrived to join Reg Lester. Detective Inspector John Dye from Norwich took charge of the Incident Room; well versed in Incident Room procedures he was another family man, stern looking, compassionate and sincere, a practical down to earth detective who, along with others, feared the worst and expected a confirming conclusion early in the investigation. Thirty-eight years later he still wonders.

The specialist scenes of crime officer and photographer was Detective Sergeant Dick Bass; cheerful to the point of flamboyance he was good for morale, but even he was subdued by the implications of the fact of April's disappearance. Very experienced in viewing scenes of major crime, his initial task was to examine April's cycle, particularly for fingerprints, and to photograph Back Lane and the adjoining area. He set to work as enquiry and search teams assembled and Incident Room officers organised tables, desks, trays, display boards and other office paraphernalia into a routine for receiving, assessing and dispensing documents. The early reaction enquiries had been unproductive – it was now to be the system, the painstaking grinding out of questions which would produce answers, which would in turn inspire more questions, and so on. Check and double check, comparison and follow-up; the detective's lot, far removed from the novelist's inspired short cut to denouement and conclusion.

Everyone being brought into the case wanted one thing, to find April Fabb; but it was a managed system of information assessment that was to be the means to an end. Individuals became a team.

The detective chief inspector from North Walsham had responded to the night-time report and was involved in the early enquiries through his territorial responsibility. On 10 April he told the press, 'We do view it in a very, very serious light.' On 11 April he announced that 'solid detective work' would begin, adding, 'I will not be satisfied until this little girl has been safely restored to her parents,' fine and hopeful words which, if intended to encourage those who waited, were appropriate. In the light of the known circumstances they were also optimistic.

In the following month, May, the detective chief inspector was to move on to retirement and be replaced by a detective from Norwich, one who would supervise the daily running of the investigation and often meet the Fabb family with Reg Lester. Reg Taylor had, like John Dye, served his detective apprenticeship in the city of Norwich, moving, after amalgamation, to the North Walsham Division. He became the detective chief inspector in charge of outside enquiries, deputy senior officer in the case. He was a seasoned detective, dour, generally unsmiling, a no nonsense officer with a reputation for thoroughness; a family man, he would undertake a competent, incisive investigation with sympathy for the Fabb family, though not seeking to match the emotional rapport and close sensitivity that Reg Lester developed. A hard and determined man he was to spend many hours with John Dye examining evidence, checking witnesses, following up information, probing theories and seeking answers. Answers that refused to come!

Figure 3.3 John Dye (centre) and Reg Taylor (right) discuss a statement in the Incident Room at Cromer Police Station. Archant (Norfolk)

The first, snap daylight search on 9 April had been unsuccessful. More searches followed, the main one immediately, in more detail; others at different times, promoted by differing inspiration and information over days, in some cases returning in later years. The first searches built upon themselves; old ground re-covered, boundaries extended, dogs thrust into undergrowth, frogmen into ponds and lakes, specialist equipment into special places – pipelines were a later example, sticks into earth – probing for a grave, and there was a physical presence inquiring into corners, crannies, crevices and buildings. In the early days it was as if the negative was disbelieved, conclusion without satisfaction leading to extension.

On that very first day the commitment was demonstrated by the appearance of a RAF air sea rescue helicopter. A request had been made to RAF Coltishall with an obliging almost instant response. Unfortunately the rescue part was not to be.

The helicopter swept across open countryside broken by tree lined roads, wooded copses and the more intensive forested areas further from Metton. It circled the fields, lanes and by-ways, hovered over the small populations of Roughton, Hanworth, Metton, Sustead, Aldborough and others, drawing attention to the sensational, almost unbelievable, the unknown. Just where was a shy thirteen, nearly fourteen years old girl, who, the previous day, had innocently embarked on a cycle ride in the country only to, apparently, disappear off the face of the earth. The helicopter found nothing.

Figure 3.4 Police display April's photograph at Cromer Railway Station.
Archant (Norfolk)

As the first full day progressed police officers formed into enquiry teams, a sergeant and three constables in each team; specific tasks were allocated, questions determined, targets identified. Transport terminals were prioritised, for while there was a presumption of the worst the art of investigation is the exploration of possibilities, the confirmation of the negative, the elimination of explanations until only the right one is left.

In a much publicised missing person inquiry it is not unusual for sightings of that person to be many and varied. In fact it would have been unusual if the police had not received reports of April being seen. They came quickly. The enquiries aimed at transport terminals found them. Two persons placed her on the three-forty pm train from Cromer to Norwich on 8 April. A passenger remembered a girl of her description on the train and the driver remembered such a girl climbing aboard. The driver of a later train, which stopped at North Walsham at six-fifteen pm, recalled a girl of April's description standing on the Norwich platform at the station.

Was it possible that April had arranged an elaborate subterfuge to disguise her intention to embark upon her coveted journey to Norwich? Would this shy, diffident, country girl have thrown her cycle in a field and carried on, by previous assignation or plan, through a lengthy walk or in pre-arranged transport, to Cromer railway station, with money unknown to her parents, to visit Norwich, either alone or with a person or persons unknown. However impractical, and detectives viewed this scenario with great scepticism, possible witnesses had been found and their information had to be followed up. Officers were assigned to travel on the Cromer to Norwich trains for several days, questioning crews and passengers.

The British Transport Police were asked to assist, and press and television appeals were made for passengers on the three-forty pm Cromer to Norwich train to come forward. Seeds of doubt had been sown in the minds of those convinced that they were looking for a body and a murderer.

There was to be a further sighting, on the following day, 9 April. A bus driver drove from Norwich Bus Station to Victoria Station, London, and a girl passenger, very like April Fabb, approached him and asked for a shilling for her bus fare. Was this the natural sequence from the train journey on the 8 April, with an overnight stay in Norwich? Was April Fabb now in London? The request for the shilling was hardly in keeping with April's normally shy disposition. Detectives pursued the information by asking for other passengers to come forward.

The press were getting off to a busy start: sensational disappearance, massive police response, appeals to the public. This was not a normal missing person inquiry. The power of television projected the drama into the homes of the interested, morbid, sympathetic, and in some cases, the downright interfering, one of whom was to be sharply exampled on the first full day of the investigation.

Late in the evening of the 9 April, as Mr and Mrs Fabb faced another night of tortured restless sleep, and detectives planned their searches and enquiries for the following day, a man was taken into custody in Metton and interviewed at length at Cromer Police Station. This fact, if known to the media, would have been projected under the euphemistic title so beloved by journalists – 'a man helps police with their enquiries': frequently incorrect because often the opposite applied.

The detained man was to be the first of many red herrings, the first of a very long line of nuisances, mostly well-meaning in an irrational way, but representative of the tremendous interest in the case and individual desires to do something practical, or what was viewed as practical.

The man taken to Cromer Police Station had attracted attention by calling at houses in Metton saying he was looking for April Fabb. Totally incomprehensible, it was inevitable that the police would be informed before he had gone too far and he was duly seized. Discovering that he was a holidaymaker staying at a Cromer hotel only added to the mystery of his actions. His movements on the previous day were checked and his hotel room searched. Nothing was found to connect him with the missing girl and it was eventually established that he had been in a Cromer café and amusement arcade at the time of April's disappearance. His explanation, that he had been motivated to assist in the search by the television coverage given to the case, says much for the power of television, and perhaps something for his own humane instincts and limited thinking.

The police, looking to the future with various lines of inquiry opening up, found fresh food for thought from two residents in Roughton. Two lady residents, from differently located addresses, reported hearing a scream just before eleven pm on 8 April. Neither was able to pinpoint the source but both asserted that they knew of night-time country noises, owls, foxes and others, and the noise was not of that type: one described it as a 'shriek', saying 'I didn't hear any vehicle or anything else.' The source of the screams was never resolved and years later a detective, by now retired, recalled them and wondered over a possible connection.

The reported screams provided more information, but no results. Room for speculation was increasing. By Thursday, 10 April, some police officers were already sensing that a long investigation lay ahead. None could forecast thirty-eight years.

Someone, Somewhere, Knows

The second full day, more searching, more enquiries; doubts whether an early solution would be forthcoming and fears whether the early searches had missed something – leading to old ground being re-covered, but still no result. More agony and waiting for the distraught parents, more speculation and conjecture, but no firm indication as to how or why April had vanished from a country lane leaving her cycle as the sole clue. How much of a clue was it? Detective Sergeant Bass examined it carefully and made a meticulous search of the area in which it was found.

The cycle was smart, new looking and in good condition. The only damage was to the bell on the handlebars, which was slightly bent, consistent with the cycle having been thrown into the field; indeed this was the only logical explanation for its position approximately six feet from the bank. The police experimented and decided that while the cycle could have been wheeled onto the grassy bank, it was unlikely to have been pushed into the field to the distance it was found because the recently cultivated earth dragged it down. The absence of tyre marks, and footprints other than Empson's, suggested that the cycle had curved through the air to its final resting place.

The cycle was repositioned in the field under the direction of David Empson. Photographs were taken, angles examined, theories proposed, with the agreed result that with the handlebars facing the bank the cycle had definitely been thrown, and not by a young girl. The most likely conclusion was that a man, of at least reasonable strength, had carried or wheeled the cycle to the top of the bank and heaved it into the field in one spontaneous action. The handkerchief, money and cigarettes remained in the saddlebag, untouched.

The dry grassy bank was firm and yielded nothing to the searching scenes of crime sergeant. The road surface was similarly unhelpful. If April had been the victim of a road accident it was a reasonable supposition that some indication would have been left on the dry surface: a skid mark, scuff marks on the adjoining bank, something from the vehicle – broken glass or Perspex, or even a spot of blood. There was nothing, in fact it was, as others were later to comment many times, as if the girl had been lifted upwards to disappear without trace. So much for the much vaunted theory of forensic investigation, which proposes that a person cannot enter or leave a place without taking something from that place and depositing some reference, however small, in that place. (The Principle of Exchange). All Detective Sergeant Bass had to work on was the cycle.

Figure 4.1 Dick Bass studies the cycle repositioned in Three Corner Field. Pillar Box Corner is in the background.
Archant (Norfolk)

A methodical fingerprint examination of the cycle revealed only one serviceable finger mark – on the handlebars. Dick Bass was too old and experienced in his trade to be carried away by the excitement of this discovery, even after he fingerprinted a jar used by April and found the resulting prints did not match the one on the cycle. Sure enough, the fingerprint on the cycle belonged to David Empson.

The scene of April's disappearance, and the abandoned cycle, had been unproductive. The investigators cast hopeful eyes towards the search and enquiry teams.

Figure 4.2 The repositioned cycle photographed by the police.
Copyright of Norfolk Constabulary

The searches, in many forms and in diverse places, continued with the obvious need to blanket an area, yet they were sometimes specific inasmuch they related to direct information or a suggestion identifying a particular place.

The main search, commencing from 9 April after the first daylight effort, was a sectional line search of countryside radiating out from where the cycle had been found, continued consistently within widening parameters through the week, the latter part of which saw cool, blustery weather with the searching made uncomfortable by sudden rain squalls. The fine weather had gone with April.

All divisions of the Norfolk Joint Police supplied uniformed officers and these were organised into teams supplemented by special constables, representatives of local organisations, civilian volunteers and RAF personnel. They trudged through fields, woods, ditches, clambered through hedgerows, slithered into copses, probed bushes with sticks, peered suspiciously into holes and hollows, stared uncomprehendingly across wide open spaces, and maintained contact with each other by sight and shouting.

Outside the main search area special places were designated for searching: Kelling Heath, Pretty Corner, Gunton Park and parts of the coast line, while others within the main search area, such as the

Great Wood, were viewed with a pessimistic suspicion that prompted detailed attention.

Caravans, camping and holiday sites, building sites and unoccupied and derelict buildings, were visited. Farmers were encouraged to search their outbuildings and the police underwater unit searched all local ponds as well as Felbrigg Lake. It was all to no avail.

Figure 4.3 Reg Lester stands where a kidnapper may have stood, flanked by representatives of the media.
Archant (Norfolk)

Searching was not totally without result, it rarely is, but what amongst the miscellaneous collection of potential exhibits could possibly relate to April? Seven handkerchiefs were found, along with the flotsam and jetsam of rags, tissues and towels discarded across the countryside by an uncaring public. One handkerchief was bloodstained and inscribed with the initial 'A'. April's parents did not recognise it, but it had to be eliminated. There followed another press appeal for information: who knew of this handkerchief?

The power of the press worked, a mother came forward to identify the initialled handkerchief and explain that it was her initial and her small son had cut his knee in the Great Wood. Another dead end! The search was proving as unproductive as the scene.

The police were progressing without result and there was no light in the proverbial tunnel, neither was there an indication of where enlightenment might be coming from.

Briefings in the Incident Room were an opportunity for exchanges of views, a chance to propose a route to solving the mystery, an opportunity to re-assess the work already done, an analysis of the lack of result. What had been missed? What could be done differently? Suggestions, recommendations for the future, followed.

An efficient Incident Room is democratic in its assessment and proposed objectives, but policy and prioritisation will always lay with the senior detectives: the detective inspector in charge of the Incident Room, the detective chief inspector in charge of outside enquiries and, ultimately, the senior investigating officer, Reg Lester. To identify with his subject he viewed a school film showing April on a broads' trip in 1968. It was a strange feeling watching the laughing girl enjoying her day out with school friends, fearing that she was no longer the girl depicted and the police were seeking her resting place.

Reg Lester informed the press that the police were keeping an open mind but this translates into 'we are not getting anywhere', well, not anywhere positive; it was just not coming together. The police could not be faulted for effort and with the public on their side there was reason for optimism. Experience had shown that the breakthrough would be sudden, leading to quick answers, a final explanation.

Reg Lester's statement, 'someone, somewhere knows something', is patently obvious, clearly true, but useful for briefing and encouragement, though countered by another of his quotes, used in briefings and lectures: the value of 'the silent witness', namely, a murder victim. The hope remained that there would not be one. But who was the person somewhere who knew something? The police needed a breakthrough.

Searchers who found nothing, experts without evidence, and interrogators without practical information: all began to wonder as the mystery remained a mystery. Where was the answer? At what point was the vital clue missed? Or was it ever there to be found? Searchers are particularly prone to self-doubt, hence the re-examination of old ground. How often is something lost and the searcher persists in returning to the same area as if doubting the evidence of their eyes? Was it there to be seen and, in a lapse of concentration, a moment's inattention, overlooked?

The conclusion of the main search, started on 9 April and concluded one week later, sounded a note of pessimism and hinted at failure. An unfair assessment if April was not actually in the search area. But what if she *was* there? On 2 May the search was recommenced using police officers only. The radius of the search was two to three miles using two teams, each of a sergeant and twelve constables. The search was intensive and recorded in pre-designated areas. The records remain today but the result was the same: nothing!

Figure 4.4 A search team confers in open country.
Archant (Norfolk)

Figure 4.5 Probing hedgerows.
Archant (Norfolk)

Figure 4.6 A haystack is dismantled.
Archant (Norfolk)

If the searches were thorough then something had been established: a negative. April was not in the countryside within two miles of her disappearance. Unless of course she had been well hidden, perhaps buried. This possibility, in the minds of searchers from the start, was in later years to take on a growing significance as attention was given to a spreading network of pipeline excavations connecting North Sea gas to the United Kingdom. In April 1969 there were none of these excavations in the search area.

Direct searching had not found her, neither had enquiries pinpointed a likely answer; it was not going to be a quick solution case, not an early discovery of a body or a revelation of a runaway from home. The 'she'll turn up' brigade were muted, the 'we'll find a body' group disillusioned. Enquiries continued, sponsored by inspiration, public information and the need to establish more negatives, eliminate the possible, the outlandish, the speculative, even a considered probable solution. But when all is eliminated and further information or theory is not forthcoming, what is left? Failure! A mystery unsolved. The police pushed on with the investigation without thought of failure.

The public appeal worked. A nineteen years old girl, who looked younger and resembled April, came forward. She had been on the platform of North Walsham railway station at six-thirty pm on the 8th and it was likely that she was the girl seen by the later train driver. But who was the girl seen getting on the Cromer to Norwich train by the other driver, and remembered by a passenger on the train? She did not come forward.

Six passengers on the Norwich to Victoria bus came forward. Two were quite sure that April Fabb was on the bus, thus supporting the driver who had reported that the girl had asked him for a shilling for her bus fare. The girl, whoever she was, did not come forward.

Figure 4.7 Police frogmen searching Felbrigg Lake.
Archant (Norfolk)

Several members of the public reported seeing April at the Easter Fair in Norwich on the 8th. There was a suggestion that April had run away to visit the fair, a theory quickly discredited by her family. She had never shown any interest in the fair, and those who knew this shy, slightly nervous, country girl would vouch that she would not singularly take herself off to the brashness and noise of a city fair.

Detectives reasoned that another April look-alike had been at the fair, but did what their job required – they investigated. Officers were ordered to track down all elements of the fair, which had by now dispersed and moved to various parts of the country. Tedious, unpromising, time consuming, necessary enquiries followed. All the staff operating the Easter Fair were traced, interviewed, and their caravans searched. The result was as expected: negative. Another line of enquiry closed.

House to house enquiries form a vital part of a major police investigation, trawling for information to be checked and cross-checked; but poaching for the insignificant which may later prove significant takes on a distorted, unreal view in a rural area of scattered population. Checking the information supplied by one household against that given by another can be of immense importance in a terraced street, but when the neighbour is two fields away it is not the same, and the nosey neighbour treasured by investigating officers becomes a rarer specimen.

The villages and widely spread hamlets of Sustead, Metton and Roughton were covered by the dragnet of a police questionnaire, presented and completed by two interviewing officers seeking new lines of inquiry or, again, that despairing routine of police work – elimination.

419 questionnaires were completed. Examined in detail in the Incident Room they provided some follow-up enquiries, which in turn gave the same result as the search teams: nothing of relevance.

In the early days, police and media activity turned the quiet hamlet of Metton into a buzzing, traffic dangerous centre of human and vehicle movement with probing reporters seeking family interviews, cameramen lurking outside number 3 Council Houses to record comings and goings, and detectives busy examining, re-examining, interviewing and re-interviewing. It was not crowded or busy by other standards, but in comparison with the normally sedate existence of those living around the narrow, twisting, sole road of Metton, it was a transformation that both reminded and emphasised the grim circumstances.

The surrounding open fields showed an imperceptibly moving line of vainly searching dots, while at the same time passing locals stopped to gossip – one topic only, and opposing cars hugged and gouged enveloping banks of earth as they struggled to pass. It was all so different to the peaceful lane that April had cycled along not so long previously.

The Fabb family stayed at home, worried and waited, acknowledged the consolation, sincere hopes and optimism (not always genuinely optimistic, for many feared the worst), and tried not to let their imagination take over. Sleep was fragmented, waking to the crashing realisation of another abnormal day, a day of stress and the agony of imagination coupled with still not knowing.

Police interviews with the family, originally briefly conducted by a variety of officers attending the scene, were now the province of Reg

Lester, with the occasional accompaniment of Reg Taylor or, even more occasionally, Dick Bass who looked for April's fingerprints, hair samples and, significantly, the identity of her dentist. Rarely would an unknown officer call on the family and when it did happen it revealed, as will be shown later, the wisdom of the known, personal approach.

The normal relationship of police officer to witness, complainant and bereaved, is the formal approach of a man or woman doing a job through impersonal procedures and training, but transposing into a humane, sympathetic person in response to evident distress, in this case distraught parents desperately wishing the return of their daughter. No police officer is cold or unresponsive to distress, but such is the nature of the employment a certain detachment is necessary to prevent a culmination of cases affecting the mental stability of the officer. Other professions are similarly vulnerable.

Reg Lester warmed to the Fabbs, felt their distress acutely, and spent a lot of time in their company. He was the first of many who would agonise along with this polite, hospitable, middle-aged couple absorbed with their family and their simple, pin clean, comfortable home with enclosing beautifully kept gardens. They, and their environment, were a world apart from the trauma, hype and competitiveness of the faster-paced living in cities and towns.

1969 was a time of rising prices, although you could still buy a new car for under £1000, a terraced house for less than £2000, and £750 was a reasonable annual salary. It was a world in which the American President, Richard Nixon, struggled with a war in Vietnam, a British Prime Minister, Harold Wilson, tried to placate strike threatening Trade Unions, and a Chancellor of the Exchequer, Roy Jenkins, prepared a budget that in a few days would sharply increase taxes. In July a man would land on the moon. All this was far removed from the enclave of anguish within which Reg Lester sought to both question and comfort the Fabb family. Not the most outspoken of men, or a confessor of inner feelings, he was later to say that he would have given anything to have solved this one case.

The greatest detectives are the general public. They are the source, the key to the police picking up the right information and, if that information is correctly analysed, checked and used, the originators of what may be described as little acorns growing into oak trees, the spark towards the ultimate result. But the public must be interested; they must be fed, kept up to date and serviced with information inspiring the willingness to help. Enter the media, the power of television, radio, newspapers.

In the early stages of the investigation, especially in a sensitive, potentially horror stricken scenario that clutches at heart strings, there is no problem. The media and public avidly consume the drama and the related distress of those concerned. But while sympathy and desire for a happy ending remains, other events compete for attention and time marches on to days when the initial impact has waned and what follows is basically an update on a non-result.

An astute senior investigator measures his investigation, drip feeds the media with information to maintain the interest, nurturing appeals and planting seeds that will hopefully kick-start a productive line of inquiry. Sometimes, such is the initial response he will merely have to go along with the groundswell of public sympathy and outrage, applying touches to the tiller to add emphasis to a particularly intriguing subject that requires developing.

The public were not only interested in the April Fabb case they were fearful of the result, outraged that such an incident should have occurred in the county where the quality of life counted for so much, and they were eager to assist to a conclusion, preferably a happy one. Reg Lester monitored the flow of information, which generally accorded with publicised progress.

Rewards manifested. Felbrigg residents combined to offer a 'substantial sum' for information that would lead to the safe return of April Fabb to her family. A Roughton woman publicly offered to add to this sum and an East Runton woman announced a teenage dance in the Village Hall, with April's friends invited and the proceeds to be donated to a reward fund. Two professional disc jockeys offered their services free for this event.

Reg Lester continued to advise the press through twice daily conferences, reduced to one and then appearing intermittently as days passed into weeks. Large posters showing April's photograph were displayed at police, bus and railway stations. This photograph, taken only the previous year at Cromer Secondary Modern School, was to become the most well-known picture in Norfolk, regularly appearing over succeeding years to highlight articles and news reports on the most astounding unsolved case in the county. It was later accompanied by the police sketch representing her hair style and clothing at the time of her disappearance.

Publicity can be a two-edged sword, one arrest had already proved this point, and the police were faced with reported sightings ranging from Curls' department store in Norwich to a newsagent's shop in Hampshire and, later, foreign countries. They could not be corroborated and remained as unresolved individual sightings made in good faith, keeping company with the doubtful identifications on the Cromer to Norwich train and the Norwich to Victoria bus.

Other reports, often anonymous, expounded theories or reported dreams, which either provided 'clues' or solved the mystery, purportedly. These reports, to be examined in more detail later in this account, tended to gather pace as the investigation moved from weeks to months, reducing as the years dragged by, but not completely disappearing as the present Norfolk Constabulary will affirm. No report or slice of information was scorned by the police, however fanciful it might have appeared on first sighting. If there was a means of checking, it was checked.

Even the most tenuous of relationships with April were investigated: a cousin who had left for Australia on the very day of her disappearance, of whom she had expressed some envy, also, a young man in Manchester who had met April when she briefly holidayed there on a rare excursion outside Norfolk, subsequently becoming a pen pal. The Australian and Manchester police conducted interviews with startled young men. Reporters particularly liked the Australian connection.

On the first Sunday after April's disappearance the Rector of Metton held a private Communion service at St Andrew's Church. At Mattins nearly half the hamlet's population of fifty-four prayed for the safe return of the girl they all knew, the girl who had herself prayed at services with her parents and had attended Sunday school there, the girl who only a few days previously had decorated the church with flowers that still survived as a poignant reminder.

Prayer and hope continued, as did police efforts encouraged by a willing public and willed on by a despairing family. Resources, expertise and organisation were powered by desire, desperation and determination: the official response was evident – continual and focussed, and unsuccessful.

In the early days after April's disappearance a small unofficial search party regularly walked the country lanes around Metton, looking hopefully into hedges already probed, across fields already crossed by an army of searchers. As light faded each evening Diane Fabb would slowly and disconsolately walk Trudy the terrier back to number 3 Council Houses, a sister and mistress still unfound. Inside the house the wild primroses were fading.

If I saw a Battleship Upside Down in a Field

Surrounded by cards and messages of sympathy and hope, Albert and Olive Fabb fought for sleep, a rest from the constant wondering, the discussions and the induced answers to different hypotheses that regularly sought to explain the tragedy that had turned their regular, comfortable lives into a nightmare. They continued the practice of leaving a light burning through the night with the front door unlocked, appealing through the media for their daughter to return under a promise of no recriminations, knowing in their hearts that their home loving girl would never have voluntarily placed her parents in such torment. For six long weeks the light burned and the door remained unlocked.

Olive Fabb told the press, 'We are hoping and praying she comes safely back to us.'

Albert Fabb tried a long shot that he knew depended upon circumstances totally inconsistent with his daughter's nature and disappearance. He announced, 'We want her to know she can come back here and not a word will be said against her.'

Reg Lester contributed to the press appeal with a message to April, saying she should 'come forward without hesitation if she should be in a position to do so'. The last part of this appeal had an ominous ring.

In the midst of this crisis of inhumanity there was much kindness and sympathy from people who identified themselves with the terrible waiting of the devoted parents. It came from people from all walks of life, people who previously had not heard of the Fabb family but now felt joined in the struggle to come to terms with the daily horror of a missing daughter, not knowing how or why she was missing.

The letters came from all quarters of the country, one envelope marked 'House of Commons' from the couple's Member of Parliament, later to call personally to express his support and best wishes; others writing to simply record their own feelings of grief and a shared sense of tragedy, or offering strength through prayer or belief, sometimes just sending sympathy as if the final bereavement was inevitable.

Each visit or approach from the police was the beginning of heart stopping anticipation. Serious looking approaching policemen are not usually the prelude to good news, but the sight of Reg Lester's brown trilby bobbing towards the front door never failed to excite Olive Fabb into the fervent hope that this was the moment when the happy ending would be announced. Courageous and optimistic, she never accepted the worst scenario, always viewing the messenger as the harbinger of joyous tidings. Alas, it was never to be and while Reg Lester and Reg Taylor were frequent visitors, Reg Lester at least weekly in the succeeding months, it was often a visit of consolation, of reassurance, a policeman powerless in the grip of a failing inquiry, faced by the very people he most wanted to help. What Reg Lester would have given to have taken good news to number 3 Council Houses, and in later years to have delivered any conclusive news at all.

Figure 5.1 Reg Lester and Albert Fabb outside 3 Council Houses on 11 April 1969.
Archant (Norfolk)

The beliefs of the parents were apparent at an early stage, manifest through the many years to follow. Albert Fabb feared the worst and in his practical, no nonsense, worldly-wise assessment of the bald facts, forced himself towards the awful assumption of foul play, specifically the kidnapping and murder of his daughter.

On 13 April he declared, 'If it is found that she has run away, we shall have to accept it. But I have not changed my mind that if she has gone away it is not of her own free will. She was picked up right enough, and I think it was two people myself. Anyone with a car had to deal with April and the bicycle.'

Few people would have argued with the father's assessment, least of all the investigating police officers.

Olive Fabb recognised the probability of the circumstances but refused to countenance the certainty that any harm had befallen April, stubbornly clinging to a mother's protective instinct that kept her child alive in the absence of evidence to the contrary. She talked of her daughter's return at any time of the day or night, saying, 'We will wake up immediately if April should come back. And that would be the most wonderful thing I can think of.'

United in their grief and fear, the parents clung to the paradoxical strand of hope that ran through their perpetual agony of not knowing. April had not been found, therefore she had not been found dead. Time was to show that the unknown can be worse than the known.

Newspaper and television reports kept the outside world in touch with their suffering and they themselves studied progress through the media, vainly looking for a life raft of information that supported their desperate desire for a happy ending. Reg Lester advised them of the police efforts and attempted to filter the determination of those who would present themselves on the Fabbs' doorstep - the press, television, freelance reporters, the well-meaning sympathetic, the visionaries, the morbidly curious and the amateur detectives, one of whom had been detained on the first night. Those who did arrive were dealt with in a charming, hospitable manner that belied the inner stress of this delightful couple. All who were to make their acquaintance in the years to come were to be visibly impressed by their pleasant stoicism. If the worst of humanity was to be the cause of this case then the very best was to be found in those who suffered from it the most.

In the early days and weeks the police remained very active, dealing with information received, conducting searches, generating their own information and suspects. The pace was vigorous and with continual new information there was every reason to suppose that, suddenly, all would be revealed.

Known and suspected indecency men were traced, interviewed, and their vehicles searched. Some were identified by previous police knowledge, others by public suggestion. Some were convicted men, others merely the subject of another's opinion based on perceived behaviour – bragging of sexual prowess, leering at girls or just generally loutish behaviour involving the opposite sex.. Whatever the reason, and however tenuous the pointer, the check was made, the alibi obtained, examined, and the relevant searches made. The anxiety to disassociate oneself from the April Fabb case usually made for ready co-operation.

On 1 May a man attempted to entice two young girls into a car at Cromer. The effect would have been serious at any time, but now it was electric and became a priority line of inquiry. He was traced to Norwich but found to have an unshakeable alibi for the day of April's disappearance. Not surprising that he was eliminated from the case, but surprising that he should have accosted young girls in an area of obvious police and media activity directed at a missing girl. Logic is often found wanting. The man later appeared before Cromer magistrates and was bound over to keep the peace.

The presence and movement of vehicles turned the police to other suspects. They held the view that a vehicle was absolutely vital to the investigation. A vehicle must have been involved. Few would argue with this view.

Suspect may be seen as a finger pointing word, a stigma, something to recoil from, leading to impulsive reactions of amazement and horror, inviting countering threats of slander, defamation, or a demand to see a solicitor, or simply a refusal to say another word – an inherent right of the British legal system that presumes silence is not suspicious. Suspect is by definition an all-enveloping word without degrees to qualify the suspicion, the origin of which may be totally subjective or general and superficial. Wonderment and suspicion can be synonymous. The police needed to know who was in the area within the relevant times: then they could be categorised. Suspects! Witnesses! Perhaps innocent, unseeing passers-by. And somewhere: the guilty person or persons.

Were they all motorists except for April? Whatever their means of travel, or their reason for being there, until eliminated from the investigation they were all suspects, if only in the loosest sense.

The police sought to turn the clock back, to re-create the day, particularly the period between and around two-six to two-fifteen pm. Everyone and everything was to be reversed back into a time capsule in which a girl cycled along Back Lane and vehicles travelled on the Metton to Cromer road.

So what, and who, was in the area?

The surveyor's van travelling out of Metton, and the Land Rover driving into Metton were known and were crucial. The surveyors tail-ended the fate of April by seeing her cycle in the field at two-fifteen, while the Land Rover driver had seen April at an identified time of two-six pm, preparatory to her cycling into Pillar Box Corner, and then into Back Lane, a few minutes away from her confrontation with somebody who had a vehicle. It is difficult to overturn this sequential account.

A Ford Anglia seen in Tom Tit Lane over a lengthy period of time was inevitably reported and this led police to the picnickers who, with free running dogs, were closest to the point where April's cycle was found. They were elderly, sleeping and negative witnesses who were still there after the cycle was seen in the field. They neither heard nor saw anything.

The remainder is a tale of two cars and two vans. The cars were seen by the Land Rover driver as he drove through Metton immediately after he had seen April near Pillar Box Corner, recalling that they were driving in the opposite direction and therefore, ominously, in the same direction as April. They were a vaguely described grey car in Metton and, turning right from the Sustead junction into Metton, a red Mini with the new type reflective number plates. Neither vehicle was ever traced. Did either of them turn right at Pillar Box Corner and then into Back Lane?

The vans received much publicity in an attempt to trace them. Although they were not seen within the vital time period they were significant, suspicious and vital to the case. They had to be traced. The first was a Ford Transit type vehicle seen in Roughton with men attempting to sell carpets. This vehicle was reportedly eliminated from enquiries in the early weeks but, such was the imbalance of publicity between the press appeal to trace it and the announcement of its elimination, to this day it is still occasionally mentioned as an important lead in the investigation. This occasional resurrection owes something to the fact that recollections of its elimination have not borne the test of time and, like the pipeline (mentioned earlier, discussed later), it is the original quest that remains in the memory. Police records show a blaze of early interest, the tracing of a like vehicle and occupants, followed by elimination from the inquiry.

The other van, a scruffy black Morris, was seen being driven recklessly through Metton and was to prove more time consuming to the police, eventually leading to a major suspect, but then, again, another reported elimination, though elimination was too strong a word in this case: lingering doubts remained for reasons that will become apparent.

The Morris van was extremely interesting because of its behaviour and occupants, and their antecedent behaviour. It was timed at two forty-five pm as it sped past the Council Houses from the Cromer direction, nearly colliding with a builder's van that had just arrived at one of the houses. It contained two men who were obviously in a hurry, something that was inconsistent with the normal flow of Metton traffic and dangerous in the narrow winding road. Although the time was out of the relevant sequence (April's cycle had been abandoned at least thirty minutes previously) such frenzied activity demanded close scrutiny.

The van's movements were further complicated by a witness who reported an identical vehicle and occupants, laughing or engaged in animated conversation, at Roughton on the B1436, also at two forty-five pm, heading towards Felbrigg. If this was the same van, and it seems very likely, it must have turned left into the Cromer road to Metton at the forked junction, and driven at a fast speed to the point where it nearly collided with the builder's van.

A further confusion of times is provided by a shop assistant and customer in the Roughton shop (the one presumed to be April's destination) who recalled a man trying to change sixpences at a time estimated to be between three and three-thirty pm. Their description of this man fitted one of the van occupants.

Although the Morris van number had not been noted as it swerved past the builder's van certain features had been observed, principally a transfer and a missing door handle, leading the police to trace and seize the vehicle. At this time it was of no use to the owner. He was in prison. To be exact it was an admitted part ownership with another man, also of criminal reputation and conviction.

Frank was a Norwich man, consigned to prison for theft after the 8th of April, something that came as no surprise to police officers who regarded him as unpleasant, unco-operative and regularly attracted to other people's property. He was to surprise them by freely admitting his presence in Metton with the Morris van, although denying all knowledge of April, or anything that might relate to her, explaining that he and his friend (accomplice would be the police terminology), who he declined to name – and still remains unknown (for certain), had been to the Aylsham Sale and had become lost in unfamiliar territory.

The police conducted a series of interviews in which Frank readily admitted visiting the shop, swerving past the builder's van and travelling various roads in the area – including the Cromer to Metton road, indicated to the interviewing officers with the aid of a map: unprecedented assistance from a man not renowned for helping the police. It was, however, a familiar syndrome in which the most anti-authoritarian person would react to the publicised concern and revulsion of a child case, seeking to disassociate themselves rather than take the in-character course of refusing any form of co-operation.

The police were later to form a strong view that the occupants of the Morris van had been engaged in breaking into isolated telephone boxes and were making a rapid exit from the area when they were observed.

What about the confusion of times? If the witnesses in the shop were right the van had returned to Roughton after the near accident in Metton. Perhaps the shop occupants had misjudged the time; but more likely they had not because Frank admitted returning to the general area after narrowly missing the builder's van, claiming that he was lost. He also admitted that his companion had gone into the shop, though he made the time much earlier, during the first journey. It was a series of times and events that never fitted properly as an ordinary travelling sequence, though as a crime prospecting expedition it seemed less strange.

If Frank had been involved in April's disappearance it is surprising that he should be hurtling through Metton half an hour after the event and then return to Roughton an hour later. On the other hand he may well have been lost for he was known as a city criminal. Another point to weigh was his unusual admission of a presence, possibly inspired by questions concerning a crime he had not committed. The police were left with much food for thought, and precious little evidence.

Police examination of the Morris van failed to make any forensic links with April. Its owner served a prison term for theft offences and was later to die at a relatively young age. Another name in the file; another product of industrious enquiries; another negative result. The police were entitled to look forward to more positive results from their efforts.

Figure 5.2 An unrealised destination.
Back Lane emerges onto the B1436 at Roughton.
In this 1994 picture the sweet shop has become a private residence

An observer, freshly drawn to the unspoilt countryside around Metton, would rightly consider the task of tracing the sporadic movement of vehicles through silent empty lanes, their drivers devoid of any reason to recall their trip, a thankless, daunting, if not impossible task. Not entirely so in a case which gripped the attention of not just Norfolk people but the entire nation as well. Many drivers came forward with details of journeys and times that impinged upon the geography of the area, sometimes recalling details of other vehicles or persons seen, thereby spawning further enquiries designed to fit everything and everybody into place, to turn the clock back to the fateful day and its critical time frame.

Some of the police enquiries strayed into delicate personal territory, not unusual when digging deeply into a person's movements. In two cases the placing of a male person at a particular address needed maximum diplomacy to elicit information that might be relevant to the investigation rather than moral issues. One such enquiry identified a man driving from Metton through Back Lane (the same direction as April) at approximately two pm, a journey of some potential embarrassment to him because of the person and place he had been visiting. He carried a suspect tag until his presence at Roughton between the vital times was confirmed.

A man visiting Hanworth was similarly disconcerted by the focus of police attention, but also quickly returned to anonymity as the police eliminated another suspect and pressed on relentlessly in their search for a more sinister figure. How the sins of one can catch up with others!

The whole of Metton was pinpointed on the day, particularly between the relevant times. Farm workers, including a tractor driver, had been in fields bounding Hall Farm and the Cromer-Metton road. At around two pm they had been frustrated by defective machinery and been joined by farmer Harrison. One of the workers left to go into Metton, on the way seeing his daughter who, with April, had been playing with the donkey. He did not see April. Farmer Harrison left and drove through Back Lane in his Mini pick-up en route to North Walsham for new machine parts, the time of his journey estimated to be after two-thirty, by which time April's cycle had been thrown in the field. A Back Lane driver could not see over the bank to where the cycle lay. If April had been in evidence Harrison would have not only have seen, but recognised her, for she lived nearby and baby sat for him.

Within this rural, sparsely populated area of minimal traffic there appeared an aid to the search for vehicles that no novelist would have dared to include in a work of fiction for fear of being ridiculed as implausible. A person taking vehicle numbers from passing traffic. Not one, but five persons over the two days of 8th and 9th April. Two boys on the Felbrigg-Roughton road, another boy on the Sustead road and two girls on the Hanworth road – a narrow little used road which also joined with Pillar Box Corner. This incredible turn of events presented the police with 406 registration numbers that in turn led to more hope, industry and disappointment.

Many of the written numbers had been recorded incorrectly, some were fictitious (juvenile cheating?) and the genuine ones that produced drivers also produced interviews that verified movements and ruled out suspects. Again the police had made progress without enlightenment.

The most notable of the number takers was a schoolboy operating from his front garden on the Sustead road, not far from the junction that would take right turning traffic into Metton. His numbers were recorded in an exercise book without distinguishing times or dates, but he recalled taking numbers from one forty-five pm onwards on the 8th. This time was to prove crucial to another man now firmly in police sights as a suspect.

Figure 5.3 Vehicle numbers recorded by juvenile spotters

Again, it was the negative that proved important, not what had been recorded but what had *not* been recorded. The red Mini with reflective number plates, which had been seen turning from the Sustead road by the Land Rover driver, and logically would have been in the exercise book, was not found. The recorded numbers did not lead to such a car.

It is an unfortunate fact of a major police investigation that those who are primarily involved in a worthy, helpful, perhaps accidental role, often distressed or confused by the experience, are subject to what are apparently ruthless police enquiries. Sometimes a considerate act is misconstrued until the true motives have been confirmed. The police take nothing for granted, neither should they for pure altruism cannot be presumed. David Empson fell into this category.

The principles of police work are not always understandable to those who resent personal enquiries and are sensitive to implication, but well understood by the Fabb family desperately hoping that the thoroughness of the police would end their personal misery. Not so clearly understood by David Empson who had reason to curse police persistence.

Empson became embroiled in concentrated police enquiries that labelled him a suspect, not because he had found April's cycle, although that was a starting point, but because a witness identified him driving a car on the Sustead road at two-ten pm, a very material time to April's disappearance. If the identification and time was right then the car number should have landed in the schoolboy's exercise book. Neither Empson's car nor one that could be related to him was there. And neither was Empson according to exhaustive police enquiries in Cromer. It was, however, an uncomfortable time for the man suddenly subject to interrogation and priority enquiry.

An analysis of Empson's actions made him a two-way loser. The act of finding April's cycle and then going to some trouble to hand it to the police was as commendable as it was illogical by the standards set by others. Whether innocent or guilty of April's disappearance, the worst construction could be placed upon his action. It was probably more illogical if guilty, though it was not unknown for murderers to 'find' their victims and, after all, Empson's were the only fingerprints on the cycle. These facts would not in themselves place the man under intense scrutiny, but a witness placing him nearby at a time material to April's disappearance, a time that ran contrary to his own account of movements – that was altogether different. It made him a red hot suspect.

The police did their job thoroughly. They interviewed with a distrusting intensity reserved for the contradictory, the storyteller thrust into the spotlight because recorded facts do not add up. Both the witness and David Empson could not be right. Someone was mistaken or lying. Police officers can be very pointed in relaying an obvious clash of stories. That they were equally diligent in checking Empson's movements in Cromer was the saving factor for this unfortunate man, now subject to rumour and innuendo from people who found it difficult to accept that someone would go out of their way to recover a cycle and take it to the police. His actions were not easily understood by many who advocated policies of 'mind your own business - nothing to do with me – do not become involved', hence the paradox of a public spirited action being construed as suspicious.

One suggestion of merit is that he had an entrepreneurial eye to the future in which unclaimed property is returned to the finder; a view sustained by his later purchase of a similar cycle.

David Empson bitterly regretted being involved, and even after the police had corroborated his movements in Cromer by using a shop till record of purchases, and interviewing customers either side of a sale described by him to apportion a time, he remained disenchanted with the turn of events. He woefully announced, 'This has put years on me,' going on to make a statement seized upon by the press with relish: 'One thing I know. I shall never help anymore. If I saw a battleship upside down in a field now I shouldn't report it.'

Gossip, which had kept pace with the renewed interest of the police in David Empson, and thrived on the old adage of 'no smoke without fire', was not satisfied and reported his recently excavated garden in knowing terms. The unhappy man publicly pointed out that he had cultivated his garden without police assistance and expected a fine crop of potatoes this year. Sadly and profoundly, he declared to reporters, 'I don't mind helping them. I have been helping them a fortnight.' This help included his car being thoroughly examined for a forensic link with April. There was none.

This much questioned man endured the rigours of suspicion through the fateful circumstances of a particular day combined with the inconsistency of his account with another. The thoroughness of police enquiries worked in his favour but he, understandably, felt tainted by the pressure.

The police, faced with conflicting witnesses, had evidence to support Empson and decided that the Sustead eye witness had made a mistake; but if so, what car had actually been seen? Empson drove a salmon coloured Viva. The witness had described him driving a new looking red car. This was unlikely to be Empson's vehicle, which would account for its absence in the schoolboy's book. But why did not another number from the book identify a red car driven by a David Empson look-alike? It was never resolved. Mystery upon mystery.

The red Mini with reflective number plates, seen by the Land Rover driver turning from the Sustead road shortly after April had been seen cycling to Pillar Box Corner, was never traced. Was it driven by a person resembling David Empson, previously seen and mistakenly identified by the Sustead witness? And within a few minutes to come upon a young girl cyclist in a lonely country lane? Conjecture then, conjecture now.

Whatever the truth, it was not to be revealed to the satisfaction of David Empson who, like the Norwich suspect, the unsavoury Frank, was to die before attaining old age, never knowing what really happened on the day that so incredibly marked his life, and seemingly took the life of another.

If Only There Were News

Days passed into weeks, then months. The press paragraphs became smaller, more occasional. Police searches became a rarity, enquiries reduced along with information and inspiration, hope faded. The Fabbs returned to work, into a semblance of their previous routine, with heavy hearts. Their agony did not diminish, if anything it increased with a dreadful realisation that whatever had happened was not to be immediately identified; there was to be no early recognition of tragedy, no formal grieving over circumstances, no last farewells. A happy conclusion now seemed as remote as the stars; even a conclusion was not forthcoming.

The suffering parents could only watch despairingly as the publicity and activity subsided, trying not to reduce the proportional expectation they had drawn from the efforts of others. The daily, weekly, public focus had gone. Their private hell of not knowing, fuelled by imagination and anticipation, levelled out from its first grief stricken impact to something they learned to live with over a longer period, and were to extend into something much, much longer.

Police investigation teams were gradually reduced in the face of declining enquiries and mounting negative results. The frustration of officers standing down while a family prayed and waited, while the public still anticipated a conclusion, was enormous; in fact, they were as near to finding the truth in August 1969 as they were in April when they started. Yet August was to be the month of a resurgence of endeavour when, disappointed but not discouraged, they reacted to the lack of new information by recalling officers to the case and going back over old ground, literally. It was the search syndrome again; had something been missed? There was a nagging doubt, the need to satisfy, even if the outcome was to be the same.

Reg Lester rejuvenated the media, stating, 'No one appears to have seen this girl speaking to anyone. No one appears to have seen her getting into a car. But somewhere, someone must know something and we ask that person to come forward.' It was a laudable attempt to kick-start the investigation into a higher gear but the detective chief superintendent must have guessed the likely result to the familiar phraseology – the same as before in terms of incisive information. The police would have to generate a new response.

Every person who had made a statement or completed a questionnaire was seen again. Anything to add? Absolutely sure? The emphasis was pronounced.

April's school friends were re-interviewed. Persons who had moved from the area since April's disappearance were traced, likewise persons moving into the area at the relevant time. Reasons for the move were examined against original answers. Again, anything to add?

The revived level of police activity provoked much interest but produced nothing of value. The number of officers working on the case was again reduced.

More assistance was offered, in an unusual form. Where rational, well tried police procedures had failed a new perspective appeared as a short cut to success. A famous Dutch clairvoyant pronounced upon the mystery and, at the behest of a television company, tendered his services. His credentials were impressive and, although the case was five months old, he was confident. He was not new to the case. He had apparently already received a vision at his home in Holland that a man aged about forty years, armed with a rifle and accompanied by an alsatian dog, using a grey/green Morris Minor car, had thrown April's cycle into the field. His description of the man included such detail as stubby fingers and fingerless mittens, a preciseness of information that caused some wonderment among those seeking material witnesses. His perceptive powers did not extend to April's fate after the throwing of the cycle.

The visionary sketched a small town, which he said the man visited. The police thought the sketched town looked remarkably like Aylsham and set to work to trace similarly aged men with stubby fingers, fingerless mittens, a rifle, alsatian dog and Morris Minor car. They were aided by a personal appearance from the clairvoyant who identified Aylsham as the correct town and announced that he expected April to be found shortly. He was wrong. Nothing was ever found to support his pronouncement and the sceptics gave knowing sighs and filed another negative enquiry.

On 2 September 1969 Reg Lester contemplated another missing child inquiry. Steven Newing was eleven years of age, last seen playing outside his Fakenham council home at three pm but not seen again. There were no clues, no positive lines of inquiry. The case never received the levels of publicity generated by the disappearance of April Fabb, neither was the flow of information so consistent over the following years; it remains another mystery, a tragedy of the unknown.

The Steven Newing case drew upon police resources, but not to the detriment of the April Fabb case in which much had already been done and, frankly, there seemed little else to do. Time, and a likely answer, was slipping away. Reassuring and comforting April's parents was becoming an exercise in faith, a continuing hope that, one day, something positive could be relayed.

While checks had been made with national cases involving missing girls, such enquiries had been seen as routine and had not excited the wilder sections of the media – not yet. Police progress had not been subjected to dramatic comparison with similar cases; there was no serialisation of the sinister, the ominous, the parallel events that might create an overwhelming sense of the unreal, unsettling the public at large, disturbing the Fabb family with fresh visions of a dreadful outcome: not until Steven Newing – a matter of increased anxiety that two young children should disappear in the same county within a few months. But even then, neither public nor press sought to criticise the police or spread alarmist stories. Sympathy and support for the police and relatives remained conspicuous.

It was, nevertheless, quite clear that new incidents caused fresh suffering for those who had already suffered. The unexplained disappearance of another child in the county, with the consequent publicity, re-lived the earlier torment for the Fabb family and raised fresh speculation among the press, public and relatives. Never forgotten, the April Fabb disappearance now had a new anvil of discussion.

Contact with the Fabb family ran the gamut of emotions, evidenced through expressions, conversations or evident behaviour. People drew comparisons, made references, offered suggestions. Some were kindly and considerate, others clumsy and tongue-tied, undiplomatic and ingenuous. Some sought the company of the parents, counselling and sympathising, others sought to distance themselves through an inadequacy of speech and personality that could not countenance contact with the most prominently grief stricken couple in Norfolk. Another publicised missing child was an unwanted talking point.

The next year was to provide another tragic talking point, much closer to home, and through the years there were to be many more in different parts of the United Kingdom. One had been broached in the first few months, when an early discovery of April, or the manner of her going, was not forthcoming.

Jane Taylor was ten years old when she disappeared from Mobberley, near Knutsford, Cheshire, on 14 August 1966. Her cycle was found abandoned in a field. The times encompassing her going were two-five and two-twenty pm. The circumstances were remarkably coincidental and the two cases were discussed between Norfolk and Cheshire detectives, the latter visiting Metton in 1969.

For those who said that April Fabb would never be found, basing this view on a first year of brick wall progress, there was to be a salutary comparison. Jane Taylor was found in a shallow grave in North Wales in 1972, some 100 miles from her point of disappearance. A further example that time only erodes and never eliminates possible success was the later detention and conviction of her murderer – not to be connected with April Fabb.

Figure 6.1 A family waits. Mr and Mrs Fabb with their daughter Pamela and grandchild Duncan, April's friend Susan, and April's dog Trudy.
Archant (Norfolk)

The season of goodwill in 1969 made little impact in the Fabb household. Their first Christmas without April; without knowledge of her whereabouts; whether she was alive or dead. They exchanged seasonal greetings and Christmas cards with new found friends, received more commiserations, celebrated the special day quietly and looked to the new year with prayer and new hope. It was to be the beginning of many such years, their hope constantly fluctuating through surges of information and corresponding police and media activity, nursed by their own faith that an answer would eventually be delivered.

The family had not been forgotten at Christmas. The press revived the case with graphic descriptions of the plight of those who remembered every day, hoped every minute.

Elder sister Pamela said, 'This is the season of goodwill. Perhaps if someone knows something, they may tell us now.'

Olive Fabb succinctly described her own agony with the publicised quotation: 'It is this not knowing – if only there was some news.' Nobody could have put it better.

There was no response. If those with answers heard, they did not heed. The New Year was no occasion for celebration of the old in the Fabb family. They went into 1970 with other stories demanding media time. The tragic story of April Fabb was lapsing into history.

Out of the spotlight, maybe, but the case had burned deep images with both police and public. The name of April Fabb was known to all. In Metton, the church notice served as a constant reminder. Like an everlasting flame, it not only cried out to those who needed no reminding, who would never forget, but also to those who visited and wondered; whether it was one week after the loss or twenty-six years later. The notice endured the ravages of weather, pecking birds and human hands, changing in format, paper protection and writing style, but always serving as a documentary beacon confirming the place and the happening. In 1995, after publication of 'The Lost Years', it was removed and its message transferred to the memorial stone that can now be found at the church entrance.

The Vicar of St Andrew's Church was the original author and he had pinned the notice to the church door within a week of April's disappearance, appealing for remembrance and prayer for the lost child and her family: not the exact wording seen by later visitors, but a similar heartfelt message. A woman visitor sought permission to reword, re-style the notice. Her offering was approved by April's parents and later written in calligraphic style by a man from Felbrigg. Encased in cellophane and pinned to the church door it was much photographed and solemnly discussed, a poignant cry to the normal world, a reminder of abnormality and continual suffering. The final sentence of the notice, carried onto the stone memorial, is straight to the heart: 'Please remember also the parents & relatives who still wait and hope.' Hope never dies in the Fabb household.

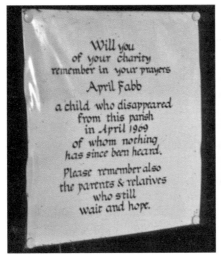 

Figure 6.2 A notice on a church door, 1969-1995   *Figure 6.3 A memorial, 1995 onward*

Among the messages of sympathy to April's parents there appeared the repetitious, those who formed a bond and reappeared over months, years, as opposed to the majority who helped them over the first horrendous realisation that no longer were they a normal, happy, closely knit family that read of dreadful events or viewed them on television; they were now part of something that was so personally awful it could not possibly have been envisaged.

The most persistent cards were postmarked 'Newmarket', received at Easter, addressed to 'Mr & Mrs Fabb' in distinctive writing and signed 'friends', appearing regularly over the early years. The friends were never identified, but they remained a source of comfort and intrigue to Albert and Oliver Fabb, until the cards stopped suddenly, without explanation.

Visitors were more obvious. They came in many forms, with differing counsels, all ostensibly related to the loss of April but not all diplomatic in their message of hope or sympathy. Some were so intrinsically wrapped up in their own beliefs, or powers, they neglected true recognition of the sadness before them. The genuine comforters, and those who offered prayer, mixed with those who professed special powers and offered answers, the latter tending to be wildly inaccurate and liable to promote more distress.

Some of the visitors were known, the Member of Parliament was one example, and practised in comforting and counselling the distraught parents. That they, and he, had taken the time, and displayed such genuine sympathy, was in itself a comfort and part restoration of faith in fellow human beings. The Fabbs were very grateful.

A regular counsellor over a very long period was a little lady, elderly, sympathetic, steeped in faith and hope, always speaking in comforting and confiding tones that endeared her to Olive Fabb. She visited weekly, initially without warning and uninvited, in a taxi, which was kept waiting outside for the hour she spent at number 3 Council Houses. Much liked and appreciated by Olive Fabb, she provided a soothing period of relaxed conversation, an oasis of close companionship that tempered the harshness of reality. Where this little old lady came from, or who she was, was never known, although her conversation gave Stalham as a clue. Her visits stopped suddenly without warning. Olive Fabb presumed, sadly, that her friend had died.

However exasperating the person or the time, and many arrived inconveniently at meal times, the Fabbs listened politely, carefully, hopefully, as theories were propounded, sympathies expressed, questions posed, interviews commenced.

The sudden appearance of a shuffling figure on the doorstep could be the prelude to a variety of topics. The spiritualist couple who travelled many miles, on more than one occasion, professed to offer guidance into the spirit world; a Wisbech man called to take the Fabbs into the past through self-proclaimed supernatural powers, and a man from Erpingham presented himself more than once to solve the case by telepathy. They were examples. There were others. All purported revelation. All failed.

Some of the others were more conformist, like the well-known television reporter who became a good friend of the family over many years. But whoever they were, they were all graciously received. Olive

Fabb was to be the dispenser of many friendly cups of coffee over a long period. She admits to only one rejection, also an ejection – the man who appeared at the kitchen door without explanation as a meal was about to be served. He wanted to ask questions about 'the case'. The case! Police terminology! It was more than just a case to the Fabbs. It was a heartfelt, personal tragedy of unbelievable enormity. Olive Fabb politely threw her visitor out, in a manner of speaking. He returned the next day and introduced himself as a policeman, his apology and newfound propriety only barely mitigating his insensitivity of using 'police-speak' on the first occasion. To this day Olive Fabb permits herself an ironical smile over the only one turned away when several others might justifiably have exited on the ample grounds their insensitive presence, manner and questions provided.

Many potential callers were deterred by the police who sieved an unprecedented mass of correspondence purporting to solve the case or offer the means to do so. Several maps, some with X marks the spot, were received and there was a proliferation of amateur investigators and know-alls, mostly using methods that bore little relation to normal police work. They were dealt with politely, if dubiously.

The police were not immune to the anguish of the Fabbs and in open-minded desperation were prepared to listen, study and act upon all sorts of suggestions and claims, some of which would in lesser circumstances have been scornfully cast to one side as the work of charlatans and cranks, as indeed many were. Letters from spiritualists, fortune tellers, dreamers, dowsers, pendulum watchers, psychics, and the just plain intuitive, were examined closely, as were the mysterious, for there always remained the possibility that a guilty person was communicating for some perverted reason.

The police were advised of April's body in Norfolk at Blakeney and Potter Heigham, among other places, and her living presence at Guildford, Oxford, Stourbridge, Leicester, and in more faraway places such as Holland, Ostend and Tangiers. The man who adamantly claimed that April was working in a night club in Toulouse was both anonymous and wrong, as was the man who insisted she was a maid in a Croydon hospital.

A sunken grave, marked on a map by a genuinely concerned, well-intentioned Norfolk man, with the courage to give his name, was found to be a concrete relic of the First World War. Other letter

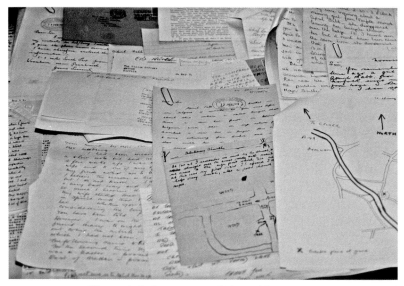

Figure 6.4 Just a part of the public response

writers made helpful suggestions concerning drains, ditches and, of course, the pipeline which networked out from nearby Bacton to serve the country. In later years the incidence of suggestions was only reduced, never completely absent, reflecting the continuing interest and desire to solve the mystery.

The pipeline was mentioned only occasionally in early correspondence and telephone calls, but later was to appear regularly as popular rumour overlooked known facts and settled upon a solution made more logical by the process of time. Although Bacton opened in 1967, the great majority of the ditches dug to receive the pipes were not commenced until later, in 1969, much of the work being done between June 1969 and January 1970. It is true excavating workmen were in Norfolk in April 1969, but they were surveying and digging connections where the main pipelines would have to cross roads. No such connections were made in the search area though they could not be ruled out further afield. Enquiries were made with the gas company and while the interiors of the pipes were ruled out by technical surveillance, the enclosing excavations required a different approach.

Twenty years later, when the press pursued the pipeline question with more vigour than their 1969 counterparts, Reg Lester told them:

'We followed up that line of enquiry extensively, using a helicopter equipped with a device which highlights the position of buried bodies.'

Helicopters had appeared twice in the search for April Fabb, the earlier one looking with more hope than the later one. Publicity and knowledge of the pipeline search was not immediately apparent and throughout the years it has remained the subject of speculation.

The broadside of solicited and unsolicited information was often generalising, suggestive as opposed to specific, trivial rather than meaningful, but it was all studied, checked and filed. If a statement could be followed up it was, but proffered Xs marked on crudely drawn maps were usually so vague, nearly always the work of an anonymous author, that the police more often than not could find no basis for a serious enquiry.

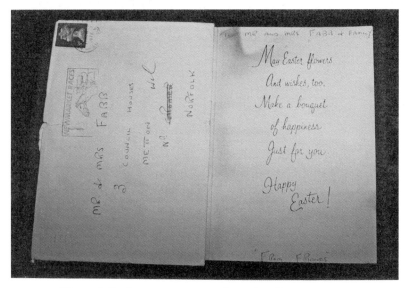

Figure 6.5 An anonymous and regular Easter message

Nominated suspects were checked: the informants in these cases not always anonymous but usually well-meaning as opposed to vindictive. The public really did want to help. Even the mistaken sightings, the confused spiritualists and like, believed they were helping in their own particular way. They clouded the issues, diverted the police and, if they became known to the Fabb family, caused unnecessary distress; but they shared a common motive to help the police and the family. It takes all sorts.

An anonymous letter to the *Sunday Express* employed the cryptic method, so beloved by blackmailers, of using words cut from newsprint to convey the message: 'link disappearance of April Fabb with Woodgate and Hazelend'. No other explanation was offered and, with no apparent relevance, the police were forced to conclude that this particular missive was more mischievous than well-meaning.

Figure 6.6　An anonymous and cryptic message to a national newspaper

Into the 1970s without discernible progress towards a solution, Norfolk people spoke knowingly of the day someone would stumble over bones, or a deathbed confession would relieve one person's torment and alleviate others. There was no discussion of a runaway girl or amnesia or just kidnapping, only the strong possibility of murder and where the victim might now lay. But no one knew for sure, except of course the person who had thrown a cycle into a field. He, and surely it must be a 'he', knew April's fate. With time marching on his secret was still firmly held.

Sharing Other Tragedies

he first anniversary of April's disappearance brought more sorrow as the Fabb family struggled to come to terms with a year of misery, a year that had taken but not provided. Their hope increased with the re-emergence of police in and around the small hamlet. During the five days of the Easter holiday police set up road blocks at Pillar Box Corner between ten am and four pm. They questioned drivers concerning their movements one year earlier and, long shot that it might have been, they found a holidaymaker with consistent habits. He was staying at a Cromer hotel, had stayed there the previous year, and had driven through Metton at Easter, just as he was doing now. The regularity and routine of the human mind is well-known to detectives.

Seemingly incredible, the holidaymaker recalled passing a girl of about fourteen years of age giving rides on a donkey to two younger children in a field. It says much for the intensity and determination of police enquiries that one year after April's disappearance they should find another apparent eye witness. That he was potentially both a witness and suspect goes without saying, but nothing was discovered that might connect him materially with the case and, disappointedly, his memory recall did not take them any further. More work, more hope, another dead-end.

The first anniversary also saw police re-visiting hotels and boarding houses, comparing lists from the previous year with current visitors. Where two Easters were recorded the visitor was interviewed and a statement describing the previous year's movements was taken.

The obvious revival of the investigation had again provoked press and television interest, but there was no further information and media activity fizzled out.

Into the second year and still no further forward, the police were now into a pattern of responding to events that might possibly relate, checking occasional information and, as they dealt with offenders in other cases, pursuing extra enquiries to establish that person's whereabouts on 8 April 1969. If the case was constantly in the minds of the Fabb family it was also never far from the thoughts of Norfolk police officers. No chance was missed to check other circumstances to see if there was a possible correlation. Officers dealing with peeping toms, linen line underwear thieves (known as 'knicker nickers'), flashers, accosters, rapists and other perverts that came to notice, had an additional task in each case, one that usually came automatically: check for a possible connection with the April Fabb case.

The allocation of extra police on the first anniversary was not only a sign of thoughtful police work in anticipating possible holidaying anniversaries, it was a sign of the almost obsessional resolution felt by some officers determined to overcome the frustration of drawing a complete blank in an emotional, much publicised investigation. Determination, application, industry: all present without reward, serving only to fuel speculation and frustration as the case refused to budge from baffling to promising. And detectives were influenced by another problem in 1970, a problem of frightful significance, the murder of a girl at Aylsham. Was there a connection? Were they looking for a double killer? This new tragedy was undoubtedly murder. Susan Long, aged eighteen years, had been strangled.

Susan Long had left Norwich late in the evening of 10 March 1970 by bus and alighted at Aylsham to walk to her home. She never arrived. Her dead body was found the following morning by a milkman in a lane off Burgh Road, Aylsham.

Aylsham is eleven miles from Metton. The Norfolk Joint Police now had neighbouring major investigations on its plate, albeit the April Fabb case was depleted of ongoing enquiries. Reg Lester moved to a new Incident Room, set up at Aylsham Police Station, and the chief constable called in New Scotland Yard. They sent two senior detectives to take charge of the Susan Long investigation.

Inevitably, the media drew comparisons and made connections between the Susan Long and April Fabb cases. The police maintained their 'open mind' response, which translated into 'we don't know'. This official response was maintained throughout the parallel running of the two cases and continues to this day because both cases remain unsolved, though not without hope, and indeed twenty-first century advances in DNA technology have produced a flurry of activity in the

Susan Long investigation.

The Susan Long Incident Room officers at least knew what had happened. It was a much publicised case, willed to succeed by horrified citizens still trying to relate to the lack of success of the April Fabb investigation one year before. North Norfolk was again inundated with police officers collecting evidence; evidence which was assessed with both cases in mind, but which persistently failed to make a connection.

The Susan Long investigation flourished and withered as the mass of information tailed off without a clear-cut result. The New Scotland Yard officers returned to London and Reg Lester and his officers continued enquiries in response to intermittent information. Susan Long became another case to check against ongoing events; a routine of not forgetting, checking for a link where none had been seen but could conceivably exist.

It is a popular belief among police officers working on a major crime inquiry covered by Incident Room procedures that the answer is always somewhere within the system: the system of receiving, processing, analysing and acting upon information – solicited, unsolicited and deduced; it just needs the vital connecting, revealing link to shout the answer to the investigators. Sometimes that shout is muted, clouded by other issues or information mistakenly, or deliberately, supplied; yet the answer is there, however well hidden: or so it is believed. This belief has often been proved right by retrospective examination of long running cases eventually solved. Where was the link missed for Susan Long and for April Fabb? Such self-examination was good for investigators, and for improving systems, but frustrating to those wondering over the possibilities of being so near, so far. Is the answer to April Fabb's disappearance hidden in the police file, even within the text of 'The Lost Years'?

The Susan Long inquiry had followed detailed index and enquiry procedures practised and preached by New Scotland Yard, not far removed from the methods used in the April Fabb case; but where did the answers lie? At what point in the mass of assimilated information was there a clue waiting to be followed to a breakthrough and definitive answer? Officers who worked on both cases felt that the answer to the identity of Susan Long's murderer was not far removed from the product of their work, perhaps just missing an important piece of evidence, or even a re-interview of a witness, or a further check on alibis, even a new perspective of certain movements. The investigation was believed to be so near and yet so far. But April Fabb? There were no such views. It remained, tantalising, so far.

The paradox of the cases was that the April Fabb investigation was frustratingly devoid of substantial clues, yet it endured through the years with continual interest and regular information while Susan Long started with more tangible evidence but lapsed into a non-productive condition with little extra information over the years; an extreme disappointment to those who sensed a successful investigation at the outset. The anomaly had been noticed before: the apparently difficult solved with lightning speed, the promisingly hopeful failing to come together and dragging on into frustrating clouds of supposition unsupported by evidence. This time, whatever the expectation, there was to be no solving of either of these cases in thirty-eight years, both floundering despite the best efforts of all concerned. To this day there remains nothing to materially connect them. In April Fabb's case there remains a great void of knowledge. Where is she? What happened to her?

One connection was made: the pain of bereavement was shared as Olive Fabb set her own grief to one side to counsel Susan Long's mother. The conversation was private, special and excruciating to two mothers who shared their individual distress, one sufferer seeking to alleviate the newly experienced pain of the other. Such spontaneous bravery epitomised the Fabb family who measured years of fear and promise with a quiet dignity that humbled many a professional caller.

In April 1970, in the midst of the Susan Long inquiry, Reg Lester received news that April Fabb had been murdered and was buried in Sheringham woods at Pretty Corner. A man in Norwich Prison had confessed to being present when she was abducted and killed, and had named her murderer.

Neither excitement nor elation attended the visit of Reg Lester and Reg Taylor to Norwich Prison. Both were experienced enough to know that confessions to publicised crimes were not unusual. The reasons for blatant exhibitionism, or a cry for help as others would put it, frequently escaped a 'two feet on the ground' police officer used to dealing in reality and having no truck with fantasy. But it is a fact of life that it sometimes happens, usually legislated for in major crimes by the senior investigating officer keeping some salient fact from the publicity machine, thereby providing an assessment tool for future interrogations or confessions.

The man confessing at Norwich Prison needed the most careful assessment. A suspect through his own mouth, with no corroborating evidence, he was, nevertheless, typecast in the role of a person who could have taken and harmed April. A habitual criminal, married to a Norwich prostitute, he was awaiting trial for a burglary committed after escaping from custody at Hellesdon Hospital. He had been sent there by Norwich magistrates following conviction for fraud and another burglary. That he was mentally unstable might be seen as a pointer to his likely presence at a violent crime, but on the other hand it might simply be a sign of muddled thinking and perverseness. Perhaps he was seeking some form of ingratiation with the authorities. Confinement was certainly not to his liking. He had escaped four times from Hellesdon Hospital.

His story was simple. Accompanied by his friend from Norwich he had been selling wood from a van and had come upon a girl on a cycle. His friend had forced her into the van and driven to Sheringham woods where he had assaulted, murdered and buried her. The confessor drew a reasonable sketch of Back Lane and the adjoining area and offered to indicate the burial place. He named his friend although at this stage such terminology must have been redundant.

The press duly reported a digging party at Pretty Corner, creating speculation that there had been a breakthrough in the investigation. Reg Lester guardedly responded to media interest by describing the digging as 'routine', and the freely talking mental patient, after pointing out the spot, was returned to prison.

Nothing was found, and much effort was put into disproving the substance of the man's confession. He was later to identify two other 'friends' as guilty parties before allocating the abduction and murder to an unnamed gipsy. The police dismissed none of his stories without first instituting careful cross-checking enquiries, even though by the time of the nominated gipsy they were sure they were being given the run-around. They did, however, remain perturbed over the vividness of the volunteered description of the murder.

Genuine belief, suspicion, and just plain well intended information were all actively sought by the police, but deviating, obstructive information designed to implicate ex-friends, or just foster a form of sensationalism, was counter productive and distracted and diverted officers from other work and, if escaping to the public, raised and condemned hopes of those who waited upon a solution. The instigator of this intensive police activity, occupying many hours, was left to his distorted fantasy world within which crime would continue to play a part. His story was substantially false; but did he actually know something?

It was not to be the end of searching at Pretty Corner. In April 1971, the police marked the second anniversary of April's disappearance by searching likely spots with specially trained dogs from the Lancashire Police. These dogs were symptomatic of the specialist training that continued to come to the fore in many aspects of police work, now extending to dogs being trained in significant roles such as sniffing for drugs or explosives. The Lancashire dogs were trained to detect dead bodies and they were used to search Pretty Corner, Stiffkey Marshes, and other specified areas that gave the police reason to believe a body could be buried there. Nothing was found.

The use of the special dogs had not detected anything but they themselves had been detected. Once again the observant press picked up on police activity in Metton, noting that Back Lane had been closed for 'road works' and police were again examining what they described as 'Norfolk's most thoroughly searched road'. They also observed the presence of Reg Lester in Metton. Failing to obtain confirmation of a new line of enquiry a local newspaper reported what had been seen, namely, that 'soil-search experts' were working in a field near the spot of April's disappearance, pushing 'special long sticks' into the soil and carefully examining samples.

Further intrigue came from the press reporting that a small hole had been dug and a lamp shone into the depth, the report noting that 'Two dogs, an alsatian and a sheepdog, were encouraged to sniff around'. This report became somewhat deflated by a police statement that it was 'routine really'. Routine? Two years on! Of course Lancashire dogs looked the same as Norfolk dogs and the press were left wondering.

In May 1971 there briefly appeared a gleam of hope, which, although quickly extinguished, confirmed continuing public interest and excited another measure of publicity. A mother purchased a small bag for tenpence at a jumble sale at Rockland St Mary near Norwich and, before giving it to her ten years old son, checked inside. She found a piece of paper with writing thereon. There was a number, name, and the address of a caravan site in Swansea. The name was April Fabb.

The power of the name caused the paper to be taken to the police where it was received with great interest, if not great anticipation – for there had been many false dawns. Checking April's writing in her school book was easy, her school satchel and contents remained untouched in

her bedroom, but the explanation lay through back tracking from the jumble sale, from which it was discovered that the paper was the product of a detective game played by two young girls, a game in which they provided their own clues. They knew of April Fabb, just about everybody in Norfolk did, and had sought to solve the case in their own child fantasy world. One of the clues had gone astray, strayed into the real inquiry where it had found the real detectives looking for April Fabb, a prime example of the impact of the case two years on. Unfortunately, the real detectives were desperately short of real clues.

In May 1973 another case linked itself with April Fabb, not through evidence but through a broad similarity of circumstances – another young girl missing without trace. Christine Markham disappeared on her way home from school in Scunthorpe. She was only nine years of age and she still has not been found. Lincolnshire detectives conferred with Norfolk detectives, and with Cheshire detectives – for although Jane Taylor had now been found, her killer, at that time, had not.

Figure 7.1 A poignant picture in 1972. At the request of the press Olive Fabb stands at April's last known place in Back Lane.
Picture by Anthony Peagam

The press noted the conference and reported accordingly. The public wondered. In later years they would have cause to wonder over more of these similar tragedies.

Figure 7.2 The sadness of the unknown.
Olive and Albert Fabb in St Andrew's Church.
Picture by Anthony Peagam

Time is inexorable and unsympathetic to failure, but not resolving one major inquiry does not prejudice others. In August 1974, a twenty-one years old girl holidaymaker was reported missing from Snettisham in North West Norfolk. Pamela Exall had been camping near the beach and had gone for a walk. She was never seen again. Whether she was claimed and not returned by the North Sea, or whether she was the victim of foul play, has never been discovered.

One thing investigating officers were fairly sure about was that she had not gone away of her own volition. In this sense she joined April Fabb and Steven Newing, also Jane Taylor and Christine Markham.

Evidentially, there was never any indication, or suggestion, that the disappearance of Pamela Exall was linked with April Fabb or Steven Newing, or anyone else, other than it was another baffling mystery.

In the same month of Pamela Exall's disappearance the Norfolk force found itself committed to another major investigation: an undoubted murder of a female, although the identity of the victim was unknown, as was the cause of death. The body was that of a youngish woman, found at Cockley Cley in West Norfolk, and her head was missing, never to be found. Neither was her killer discovered. There was an inescapable tragic irony in finding a female body that was to remain unidentified at a time when April Fabb and Pamela Exall remained untraced.

Mystery sometimes creates more mystery, circumstances occur that are suggestive without being revealing to those already puzzled by the main event. Two days after Pamela Exall's disappearance a tenuous link with April Fabb appeared at a well respected public house at Dersingham – not so far from the place of Pamela Exall's last reported sighting. Detectives were handed a worn newspaper cutting of the April Fabb case, carefully folded and creased as if carried in a wallet, found on the bar room floor shortly after three middle-aged men had departed. The reason for this carefully preserved cutting, describing a five years old case, being in the area of a similar case was never established. Thoughts that the men were police officers or reporters were not confirmed. They were never traced. Perhaps they were not connected and the cutting belonged to someone else. Even so, the questions remained: who had kept it? And why had it been so carefully preserved? And dropped in the area of a similar mystery! More unanswered questions catalogued for future reference. The long arm of coincidence could conjure up some erratic presumptions.

The April Fabb case never languished for want of resources, whatever was happening elsewhere, although the publicity of other horrific crimes, especially those involving females, did little for the confidence of the waiting Fabb family. Each time such a case made news, usually via a blaze of publicity, they not only wondered if there was connection with the loss of their daughter, but also their thoughts automatically went out to those who grieved or waited, torn by the horror of the known or tormented by the spectre of the unknown. The Fabbs knew all about the unknown.

With the passing of the years there was to be new trauma for both the Fabb family and the police. Norfolk was not to be rested from the publicity of violent, unnatural death.

Heidi Reddin was fourteen years of age when she disappeared from Downham Market in December 1976. The police were fearful of publicising her as a missing person knowing that the media machine would join her with April Fabb, Susan Long, Pamela Exall or the headless body, even the boy Steven Newing, possibly creating the image of a maniacal killer on the loose. Of one thing the police were sure: the possibility of any of the cases being connected was remote.

The disappearance of Heidi Reddin was a matter of great concern, but it did not have the mysterious overtones of April Fabb's last recorded moments. Nevertheless, it was extremely ominous. Heidi had been expected to take a taxi to see her boyfriend but had failed to do so and, as events were later to prove, had hitch hiked instead. Although she was much more extrovert than April, she was unlikely to have voluntarily left home leaving her parents desperately worried. The police pursued many avenues of inquiry before, two weeks later, publicising her as a missing person.

The speculation, and inevitable comparisons with April Fabb and others, continued for another month, almost to the point where there was a half expectation of another indeterminable mystery of a missing Norfolk girl, but then fresh impetus was given to the discussion. Heidi's body was found in a ditch approximately two miles from her home. She had been raped and strangled.

The case was six weeks old in missing person form (and Heidi had clearly been dead for all of that time) but now it was a newly constituted murder investigation. The chief constable called in New Scotland Yard, the last time such a call was to be made by the Norfolk force. (A parity of expertise between provincial forces and New Scotland Yard was arriving from nationally governed training). That this historical call was unnecessary, and the amount of time for further media comparisons with April Fabb was restricted, was due entirely to the rapid work of Kings Lynn detectives who moved into a suspect list of sex offenders and consequently arrested the murderer before the London detectives arrived; a matter of some satisfaction to those concerned.

The decade of the seventies moved towards the eighties with a grieving family sharing other tragedies, consciously associating themselves with other publicised bereavements, knowing that they still had the support, sympathy and the determination of others. What they did not have was the knowledge they so desperately craved: where was their daughter and sister?

The Changing Times

The decade of the seventies saw April Fabb still in the public eye. No longer a regular news item she, nevertheless, continued to excite interest as press and television coverage returned to the mystery at intervals.

Her family still waited, prayed, hoped, and patiently dealt with probing outsiders.

The police still visited in the form of Reg Lester who would take tea with the family as he reaffirmed a professional resolve to continue all necessary and possible enquiries. A very sincere man, he meant what he said and the family knew it, respected him for it.

The media continued to make trips up the garden path (sometimes metaphorically) for interviews, never refused, either making a documentary programme, writing an article of remembrance or mystery, or seeking to embellish another news story by cross-referencing to April Fabb.

Steven Newing, Pamela Exall and Heidi Reddin had provided opportunities for comparative journalism within the county, and Jane Taylor and Christine Markham had served the same purpose nationally. This vein of journalism was, sadly, never to be short of similar cases.

In August 1978 the April Fabb case was highlighted by tragic circumstances of uncanny similarity. Comparison was automatic, alarming, chilling, in no way diluted by a distance of more than two hundred miles.

Just as the people of Devon had been aware of April Fabb in 1969, so the people of Norfolk took note of Genette Tate in 1978. Like April, she was thirteen years of age, and on an August day she was conducting an afternoon paper round in the quiet village of Aylesbeare, a place not dissimilar to Metton. After talking with friends of a similar age she cycled ahead to deliver a paper. As her friends rounded a bend in the road they saw her cycle lying in the road, papers spilled to the ground. To date Genette has not been found.

The press reported upon the similarities of the two cases and Norfolk detectives discussed them with Devon detectives, more in routine open-mindedness than any strong belief that they were connected. That the same person was responsible for abducting both girls would not have surprised detectives in Norfolk or Devon – there were obvious similarities that could not be ignored, but the one overriding, unwanted similarity was the absence of clues in cases in which a young girl had vanished, with the manner of her going being a matter for speculation, and the person or persons responsible remaining unknown, undescribed, not indicated by clue, reference or logical deduction.

Geographically the area around Aylesbeare resembled that around Metton: pleasant, sparsely populated, yet close to an A class road and seaside area, midway between tourist towns (Exmouth and Sidmouth), and only a few miles from a city (Exeter).

Genette had disappeared on a Saturday afternoon, near a Bank Holiday period, in a holiday area, from a country lane. She had been cycling and been swept away within a very brief period of time. Much of this coincided with April.

An intensive police search and investigation did not find her or the person who had taken her. Like April, there can little doubt that she was taken rather than went voluntarily.

This new case re-emphasised the grief of the Fabb family. They consoled each other with the glimmer of hope that a successful conclusion to the Genette Tate investigation might correspondingly throw light upon the loss of their own daughter and sister. It was not to be. Coincidence was registered, comment guarded, and hope controlled. After all, there had been many disappointments.

The pain of not knowing was constant to the family, intermittent to a caring public, but also, in a haunting mood of frustration, a cross for the police to bear. How long could it continue without an answer? The tenth anniversary came and went, marked by a commenting press, recalled with undiminished sadness in the Fabb household. Perhaps there was to be no end. The 1970s had seen much investigative activity but the 1980s arrived with no conclusion in sight.

The entry of this new decade was to see an incident that demonstrated the sensitivity of the police to the April Fabb case, a clear indication that she was still very much to the forefront of police thinking.

On 24 October 1980 Reg Lester received a frightful message: a fourteen years old Metton girl had been reported missing. She had boarded the school bus to attend Cromer High School but had not arrived in school, and had not returned home that night. It was the bus that April had used, the school, now renamed, she attended. Another Metton family experienced a night of foreboding, reminiscent of the Fabbs' anguish over eleven years earlier.

Surely, not again! Sensation and alarm predominated. The police anticipated newspaper banner headlines with television camera teams and reporters traipsing the area, exciting public interest towards hasty, possibly unfounded conclusions. The police set up an Incident Room, quickly and fearfully.

Cromer Police Station was again the scene of furious activity as the police organised their system and instigated enquiries, starting with checks at bus and railway stations – a familiar route leading to familiar places, except that the officers concerned were following in the path of predecessors moved on to other things; retirement in some cases.

Reg Lester was the factor common to cases old and new, but this time any feelings of apprehension that he might have entertained were soon quelled. This time all was well. The girl was found, having spent only one night away from home.

The 1980 missing girl had voluntarily missed school, and her home, spending a night in local stables as she struggled to cope with her mental pressures. Not exactly a new and unfamiliar set of circumstances as young thinking attempted to cope with more mature requirements in a pressure growing world. Indeed, the young lady was not actually found; she turned up at her home having had a considerable amount of thinking time.

The police would certainly have been concerned and made enquiries into this type of missing person report wherever or whenever it occurred. But this one was obviously different, venturing towards emotions of incredulity and apprehension. April Fabb made that difference. The newly reported girl came from Metton, a place that, because of April, made all the difference. A rural unknown had become well- known, a focus and symbol of something terrible. Anything that happened in that area was going to be viewed through April Fabb context spectacles.

Those who chose to identify the 1980 circumstances with April's disappearance found no common ground, other than the obvious that had electrified the police in the first place. April had no known pressures, and if she had engineered her disappearance she had found someone to throw her cycle into a field. And eleven years is a long time to lay low pondering upon matters.

The 1980s produced new tragedies for assessment alongside April Fabb and Genette Tate, and others, starting in 1981 in Northern Ireland. Jennifer Cardy, aged only nine years, cycled to see a friend but never arrived. Her cycle was discovered thrown over a hedge. Six days later her body was found a few miles away, near a lay-by. She had been murdered. The 80s would go on to reveal more murders of young girls, in different places, all hundreds of miles from Norfolk, and this decade would also point to the existence of a serial killer.

In 1983 Reg Lester retired from the now named Norfolk Constabulary. He said *au revoir* to the Fabbs rather than goodbye. From tragedy had come friendship, and they would meet again under the auspices of the police. He took with him a great personal regret that the police had failed to find April Fabb.

The new head of Norfolk CID, the author of this book, automatically inherited the responsibility for unsolved cases within the force area: April Fabb, Steven Newing, Susan Long, Pamela Exall, the headless body at Cockley Cley. Only Susan Long and the headless body were shown as murders, the others remained as 'missing person' files, which may say something about statistics.

Reg Lester's successor also inherited a handkerchief, ten Player's Weights and fivepence-halfpenny, a vivid reminder of publicity fourteen years earlier. Reg made arrangements concerning another potential exhibit still held by the police. A BSA Star Rover cycle was sold in accordance with the parents' wishes. They, understandably, did not wish to see it again. Ownership of the cycle was not made known to the auctioneer and somewhere a young person unknowingly acquired the most famous cycle in the county.

The departure and succession of Reg Lester had no material meaning to the April Fabb investigation, for the Agatha Christie concept of individual detectives solving cases is far removed from the true nature of detective work. Organisation, method and team work are corner stones of a major crime investigation. The man in charge prioritises, inspires and decides, but he is as strong as his weakest link, or unfortunate circumstance. Pointing in the right direction is not the same as getting there. Reg Lester did, however, have inner knowledge of the case and now he was gone, along with many others who had worked and contributed to the investigation. Reg Taylor had already retired. John Dye would retire before very long. New faces were looking into the mystery of April Fabb, the old team were moving into history.

In the 1980s the police were improving organisational standards and dealing with serious crime in practical, methodical terms that did not decry the earlier years but instead marked the path of progress. Unfortunately, progress was not always united. Over forty police forces pursued their own individual improving road, which ignored the salient fact that criminals neither knew nor cared about force boundaries. Major crime that traversed these boundaries could cause differences in viewpoints. More importantly, cross-border crime sometimes threatened to bring about a joining of unjoinable investigative systems. Enter the new national systems: firstly MIRIAM, later HOLMES – the computerised way forward.

The question posed on several occasions is whether the MIRIAM or HOLMES systems would have made any difference to the April Fabb case. It will never be answered, but the reader may have an insight.

MIRIAM was the acronym for 'Major Incident Room Index and Action Management', a system that not so much improved expertise as polarised and nationalised it. It brought about dedicated training, identified special duties and responsibilities, and ensured that, when properly employed, a relentless gathering and grinding of information fell into a recognised system in which police expertise was refined by officers who had been trained and harnessed into defined roles. It was, without doubt, progress.

Selected officers were still learning the new system when a sub-postmaster was murdered at Bradwell, near Great Yarmouth. It was Reg Lester's last big case and it was successfully concluded with the arrest and conviction of two local men.

The first MIRIAM Incident Room was set up at, of all places, Cromer, in November 1983, after a local shopkeeper was brutally battered to death. Fourteen years after the April Fabb Incident Room at Cromer Police Station this new information gathering system swung into action at a Cromer hotel (redundant in winter). The local community were again involved in a massive police operation. This time it culminated in the arrest of two local men who were convicted of murder and manslaughter.

The system had worked. The 1983 Cromer Incident Room was used as a role model to demonstrate the new procedures to senior officers in the force; however, those practically involved knew that the system had worked because two detectives did their job thoroughly when checking an inconsistency of times revealed in certain statements. The system provides, but the officer on the ground has to conclude. An open goal is one thing, scoring is another.

HOLMES followed MIRIAM, improvement upon improvement, essentially a computerised system geared to the growing number of cross-border incidents that required independent police forces to operate with the same understanding, the same procedures. The name stood for 'Home Office Large Major Enquiry System'. It still works today. Whether HOLMES would have advanced the cause of the April Fabb inquiry is conjecture. One thing is absolutely certain: no system can be successful, computerised or not, if the relevant information is not obtained. No one can build without material. Crystal balls have no place in police work.

Those charged with continuing the April Fabb investigation were not allowed to dwell upon history. Unsolicited information continued to flow, promoting the necessary follow-up enquiries; and press interest occasionally surfaced as tragedies occurred elsewhere or editors sought to titillate readers with fresh articles upon a time logged mystery. After all, they still wrote of the *Mary Celeste*, Bermuda Triangle and Lord Lucan.

Still in 1983, there was an unwanted development in the case. Another amateur detective appeared, one who went to disturbing lengths and epitomised the unhealthy fascination that some people derived from the continuing mystery. He committed the cardinal sin of upsetting the family in what was an obsessive attempt to interfere, although he used the word 'investigate'.

This man, born in the same year as April, wrote from Yorkshire, initially to Pamela, and later, after he received no reply, to Mr and Mrs Fabb. In a letter of misspellings and grammatical inconsistencies he advised the parents that he had made progress in his investigations and had 'opened up new possibilities' overlooked by the police. He now sought to obtain further information from the family.

Mrs Fabb wisely passed the letter to the police who were extremely interested when they found that the writer was a man with a discreditable past, which included offences of assault and indecent exposure. Norfolk officers went to Yorkshire and confronted this apparent poacher turned gamekeeper. They found that the man had not only written to the family, but to various newspapers, a library, shipping company and Australia House – all in the cause of gathering information to prove that April had left the country, voluntarily.

His obsession had commenced with the purchase of a lurid paperback book called 'Weekend Book of Ghosts and Horror', which contained an account of the disappearance of April Fabb. From then on he had set out in his distorted way to amass a file of information and the detectives found sheets of foolscap paper depicting his deliberations. They included newspaper cuttings, letters, photographs, equations purporting to determine solutions, sketches, maps, summaries, a table of 'evidence', and perhaps the most obsessional pointer of all: his poem entitled 'April Fabb'.

Figure 8.1 The years roll by and lonely sentinels stand over an unchanging scene. If trees could only speak

The obsessed Yorkshireman could not be connected with April's disappearance, in fact it appeared that he had never been to Norfolk, and he was cautioned in forthright terms not to bother the family again. Nothing more was heard from him, except in Yorkshire.

The years rolled by, still the case occupied police and public attention. Information from interested observant citizens placed April as alive in Southampton and dead in Sizewell Power Station. The first from a sighting, the second from an overheard conversation. Both were discounted, but overheard conversations were to lead to many false conclusions as the case remained a subject for discussion. One eager informant reported that April had been murdered by a police sergeant – the result of an overheard dialogue in a public house in which the sergeant had expressed an opinion and had been seriously misinterpreted.

A telephone message referring to the case was indistinct but mentioned 'Ann Watchem' as being involved, later interpreted as 'and watching'.

Information was received from a man that, while pursuing his love life in a car parked in a lonely spot near Norwich Airport in 1969, he had found his ardour tempered by an overpowering smell, which he later allocated to a decomposing body. His belief that the experience may have been connected with April Fabb reflects the public knowledge of her name, but does not explain why it took until the 1980s before the police were given the opportunity to investigate the phenomenon. Their investigation took an interesting turn when the sensitively nosed informant was found to have visited Metton during the course of his employment. Discovering that he had a silver grey car in 1969 caused further interest. He was interviewed very closely and the site of his affair, now enclosed by the airport perimeter fence, was inspected in detail. Nothing was found and he could not be connected with April, and the cause of the smell can only be presumed along with the reason for his dilatory report.

The police continued to receive nominations for the murderer of April, along with descriptive dreams which pointed to shadowy abductors and indistinct resting places. The nominees were checked, in one case suspicion had been allocated after a suicide, and the dreams studied and filed. The head of CID occasionally visited Mr and Mrs Fabb, assuring them that the police would never give up, noting their own continuing resolve and leaving with a favourable impression of quiet dignity and courage – much as others had done before him.

Other visitors continued to appear at the Fabbs' home, sometimes unannounced, sometimes expected; the cross section as before except for two remarkable additions from outside Norfolk. The first was the astonishing arrival, just before evening meal time, of a man who identified himself as the stepfather of Genette Tate. If he was who he said he had travelled more than 250 miles, without warning or pre-correspondence, to speak to Albert and Olive Fabb upon matters of the future rather than the past. He had ideas, which he made apparent, not strictly related to Genette's disappearance. This was not a counselled meeting of grief seeking a shared bereavement. It was a one-sided, rather indulgent look into matters touching upon tragedy. The Fabbs listened politely to his views and, a little confused, eventually bade him farewell. He never returned or contacted them again.

Next came two unscheduled and disturbing visitors. Another man from Devon, a clairvoyant, was accompanied by a man from Banningham in Norfolk extolling the capabilities of his friend. They said they wished to help and were received with an undeserved courtesy, which remained unshaken when they requested a photograph of April in order to detect her whereabouts. After promising much, including their own return, they left.

The police aborted the duo's future plans. The clairvoyant announced that he had deduced from the photograph that April was dead and had been buried at Matlaske in Norfolk. His friend had by now decided that he also possessed special powers and said that a member of a football team, the photograph of which was displayed in a Norfolk public house, had witnessed the burial.

The patience and composure of the police in dealing with the visionary pair were exemplified by careful enquiries, which included an interview with the indicated footballer. The eventual result was a warning to the visitors against further intrusion into the private lives of the Fabbs. The Devon clairvoyant was not heard of again and his mentor retired into a mental hospital.

The power of the name of April Fabb extended into the late 1980s as informants, well-meaning and mischievous, continued to advise the police of the facts that they thought had been missed; how she had disappeared - and why; where she had gone - and was now; who had taken her - and where that person was now, or simply, why she had elected to run away of own accord. This latter assumption ignored or was ignorant of known facts that discounted the theory of a voluntary disappearance.

Several informants chose to concentrate upon the believed incontrovertibility of their own information to the total exclusion of all else. One self professed dreamer with great descriptive powers changed the weather on the fateful day of 8 April from gloriously sunny to overcast with steady drizzling rain, even attributing dialogue to April as she said goodbye. The police read, noted, checked and filed. Each was added to the great army of self-acclaimed know-alls. But as Reg Lester would have said, 'someone knew, somewhere!'

Strange coincidences tended to rouse police suspicions, such as the man who identified April's murderer as a Cromer hotel porter, the informant himself providing the interest because he had previously been involved in the Jane Taylor case in Cheshire as a searcher and potential witness. Neither he nor the porter was found to have anything to do with April Fabb's disappearance. His motive for contacting the police after all these years remained unclear (as in many others), and the police could only marvel at the lengths to which some attention seekers and blatant exhibitionists would go.

From Hertfordshire came a telephoned message to Cromer Police Station. The man knew what had happened to April and, furthermore, knew where she was now. A multitude of such messages had been aimed at the police since 1969, but this man spoke rationally, confidently, with some apparent inner knowledge. Norfolk detectives made haste to Hertfordshire. The story was straightforward. April had been kidnapped, taken to Jersey and subsequently to the Middle East, where she was now. The man had an informant who would reveal the exact whereabouts very shortly.

The storyteller also had a mental history, a vivid imagination and a propensity to minding other people's business, of which his interest in April Fabb was but one example. He was another who had written to a local newspaper to obtain press reports to add emphasis to his story, though perhaps this should have been unnecessary because he was in Norfolk between 1967 and 1970, a fact of interest to detectives. Again, a potential witness turned suspect was ruled out.

Another wasted journey, another unbalanced time waster latching onto a then nineteen years old case for reasons that defied logic yet continued to prove that time and distance were no bar to the fascination of the April Fabb mystery.

The changing times had seen April's parents alone at 3 Council Houses with all its reminders as Diane married and Trudy, the little terrier, died without seeing her mistress again. In retirement Albert Fabb obtained casual employment with farmer Harrison, a long ago casual employer of April and himself not far from the known events of a critical day in the history of Metton. Each day the surrounding landscape reminded all who knew and had been so near. But now time moved to a new phase.

In 1987 April's parents moved from number 3 Council Houses, leaving a sorrowful collection of memories: the long unused bedroom, carefully tended gardens with flowers that had bloomed over many years, the lawn where a young girl and her dog had played, the driveway along which that girl had cycled out of the view of her mother for ever, a house with a history, family memories, a monument to a tragic past, but a past that would not be forgotten as keepsakes and treasures of a long lost daughter were moved to the new bungalow near Cromer. A doll and doll's house, a brush and comb set, and a school satchel were given places in a new home.

*Figure 8.2 April's treasured doll's house; moved to a new home
and still retained within the family.*
Picture by Anthony Peagam

The Evil That Men Do

During the course of the April Fabb investigation a number of similar cases countrywide had been compared for possible links, without result. Now, in the 1980s, there came a horrifying list of abductions and murders of young girls, and at a time when senior detectives of all forces were receiving training in the command of joint investigations, their decision making to be allied to the burgeoning HOLMES computerised system of recording and dispensing information. The police forces of Norfolk, Suffolk and Cambridgeshire were soon to be tested by two horrific cross- border crimes, each prompting a recall of April Fabb's disappearance. The Norfolk Constabulary linked through the HOLMES system with Cambridgeshire in the first investigation, with Suffolk in the second, the cases occurring within a few months of each other. The year was 1985.

Before the two East Anglian cases came two accounts of abduction and murder involving young girls elsewhere: the disappearance of eleven years old Susan Maxwell from an England/Scotland border village in July 1982, and one month later the discovery of her murdered body 250 miles away in a lay-by off the Uttoxeter to Stafford road; then the murder of five years old Caroline Hogg, taken from near a fairground near Edinburgh in July 1983 to be found ten days later close to a lay-by near Twycross in Leicestershire, nearly 300 miles from the fairground. These appalling acts justifiably caused national revulsion.

Four police forces were initially involved in these long distance abductions and murders, and two different judicial systems. The two forces covering the abductions, Northumbria, and Lothian and Borders, formed a joint investigation. The forces of Staffordshire and Leicestershire, where the bodies had been found, supplemented the investigation and other forces would soon have a role to play. An

Assistant Chief Constable in the Northumbria force was appointed to command and co-ordinate the joint investigation, retaining that command as he moved to the Lothian and Borders force as their Deputy Chief Constable. In 1985, struggling with an unpromising investigation, he visited Norfolk to confer with the Norfolk head of CID, with good reason.

Norfolk detectives had noted the murders of Susan Maxwell and Caroline Hogg and wondered. Could April Fabb have been taken by the same person? Was she also lying somewhere in the Midlands? Near a lay-by? It was all speculative. The question was how many monsters were out there doing these foul deeds to young girls? Experienced, hardened detectives had no illusions: there existed perverted men who would commit unspeakable acts upon children, including murder. Two examples were about to appear close to home. The two 1985 East Anglian cases gave rise to more uncomfortable speculation as to the fate of April Fabb.

It was a beautiful summer's day in July, hot and cloudless. The school holidays had started and two thirteen years old girls responded to the weather by cycling into the attractive countryside surrounding Fulbourn, a small village near Cambridge. They did not return home and their cycles were found abandoned in a secluded woodland track. Such similar circumstances to the disappearance of April Fabb would have initiated a prompt inquiry of the Cambridgeshire force by Norfolk officers, but in this case it fell to the Norfolk force to advise their Cambridgeshire colleagues of the discovery of the girls' bodies. They were found late that night in Thetford Forest, left for dead by a rapist convinced that he had silenced them forever.

That the Cambridgeshire girls lived to tell their tale was a miracle of faith and determination, also a miracle of medical science in the eyes of the surgeon who brilliantly restored them to health. In strict medical terms they should have died. Their injuries were seen as non-survivable, yet they survived to confound their assailant. If they had not would an unfathomable mystery have been written into Cambridgeshire history with the answer seventy miles away? Would these young bodies have faded into Thetford Forest? Or would a chance walker, dog owner, ornithologist or rambler have discovered them? And if found, would their killer have been identified?

It was inevitable that the Cambridgeshire case of 1985, in which all the facts were to become known, would be compared with the Norfolk case of 1969 in which very little was known. Had something similar happened to April Fabb?

The Cambridgeshire girls told their tale that same night, despite appalling life threatening injuries caused when one was transfixed into the ground by a sword through her heart, and the other was run through the throat with the same sword. Their courage, combined with their miracle of survival, was to provide information showing that their cycle ride had ended with a confrontation. A sword wielding man had threatened and forced them into a Volvo estate car before taking them on a journey of terror, which detectives were later to prove lasted more than eight hours, covering four different counties, during which they were both savagely assaulted. The end was inevitable, to be admitted by the man who had taken and abused them: they were the living evidence against him, they had to die and, as he calmly told interviewing officers, he drove away from Thetford Forest believing they were dead. He was amazed that they lived. One of the girls, close to death, had crawled from the forest to a road to be found by a late night motorist.

Because of the girls, their story, their remarkable resolve and attention to detail, detectives had a lot of information to work on. Incident Rooms were set up at an Army camp in Thetford Forest and at Cambridge, combined under the HOLMES computerised system, with the Norfolk head of CID in charge.

The case drew enormous interest from the national press, but their freedom of speculation was quickly curtailed by the rule of *sub judice* – the restriction upon detailed and speculative reporting when a person has been charged and is within the province of the courts. A man was arrested and charged.

Success had been rapid. A female detective in the Norfolk force recalled that a known indecency man living in Cambridgeshire had recently been seen in Norfolk. A check of his house showed a Volvo estate car in his drive. Inquiry translated into action. Norfolk and Cambridgeshire detectives carried out an early morning raid on his house and recovered a sword from the loft, along with significant pornography. Terence Pocock was taken into custody; a detention from which many hope he will never be released. Forensic examination of the sword and his estate car made his position impossible and he pleaded guilty at Norwich Crown Court to attempted murder, kidnapping and rape. He was sentenced to life imprisonment five times.

There was no evidence connecting Pocock with April Fabb (he was 23 years of age in 1969) but police officers pondered upon his evil chronicle of assaults with a sidelong thought that it might have been such a person who met April in Back Lane in 1969.

Reflections upon the debauchery and utter cruelty of Pocock were shortly to be matched, even surpassed, by another man with Norfolk connections but living outside the county. Gary Hopkins lived in Bedfordshire, but he visited Great Yarmouth in September 1985 and was responsible for one of the foulest deeds to come to the notice of the Norfolk police.

Leoni was only three years of age, a happy excited toddler immensely enjoying a holiday at a seaside caravan camp. Due to a mistake with an arranged babysitter she was, late one evening, left alone in the caravan, and was snatched through the window and spirited away into the night. The hue and cry that followed was channelled through an Incident Room set up at Great Yarmouth.

They found Leoni five days later, seventy miles away, floating in the river at Mildenhall in Suffolk, naked, with her hands tied behind her back. She had been raped and thrown into the water to drown. Two detective chief superintendents met on the river bank, the heads of Norfolk and Suffolk CIDs, gazing sorrowfully into the slowly moving water as it caressed and gently moved Leoni in the most peaceful contrast to the violence that had cast her into the murky depths. What kind of person could have perpetrated such a deed?

HOLMES was the investigating system used by both forces, and the discussion between the senior detectives of Norfolk and Suffolk as to who was to lead the investigation was resolved when the pathologist announced that the little girl had drowned. She had, therefore, been murdered in Suffolk and that force opted to head the inquiry. The already formed Incident Room at Great Yarmouth was joined to an Incident Room at Mildenhall, both controlled from an Incident Room at Ipswich. The weight of the Norfolk and Suffolk forces was thrown into the case with the head of Suffolk CID in charge.

Gary Hopkins was not caught quickly. Everything did not come right in a matter of days but over a period of months, with credit going to the HOLMES system joining vital clues, principally due to astute management by the Suffolk head of CID who paid due attention to similar facts and connected an Essex kidnapping in which a young girl had been abandoned in Great Yarmouth. Even then the answer would not have appeared without pertinent intelligence from a Norfolk detective and, the most important and crucial factor, an incisive interview by a Bedfordshire detective who refused to accept a proffered alibi. Hopkins fell to a combination of detectives on the ground, the man at the top – and the system. He could not, however, be connected with April Fabb (he was only 12 years of age in 1969) and went to his sentences of life imprisonment as another example of degrading human low-life. Many police officers wished him and Pocock all the worst in prison.

The hackneyed phrase that 'no news is good news' had no place so many years on from 1969, and there was plenty of room for the fear that a person or persons of Hopkins and Pocock's ilk was responsible for the loss of April Fabb. And the Susan Maxwell and Caroline Hogg murders, although a long way away, were still unsolved and unquestionably the work of someone of similar disposition. The deputy chief constable in charge of the Maxwell and Hogg cases visited Norfolk to examine Pocock's possible connection. Soon he would have another case to study, which he at first doubted was connected with the Maxwell and Hogg murders. He was to change his mind.

In March 1986, Sarah Harper, aged ten years, disappeared on a trip to a corner shop in Leeds. Six weeks later she was found in the River Trent near Nottingham, murdered.

The Susan Maxwell and Caroline Hogg abductions were a very long way from Leeds, but the girls' pathetic, misused and abandoned bodies had been found within a twenty-four mile radius that now included poor Sarah Harper. It became known as the 'Midlands Triangle'. The Sarah Harper investigation was joined with Susan Maxwell and Caroline Hogg. A wise move because the same man killed all three!

8 April 1989 was the twentieth anniversary of April Fabb's disappearance. The image of a fair haired smiling girl saying goodbye, riding out of the family drive on a sunny day, could never be repeated. Time had taken a life away. If April was alive she was approaching her thirty-fourth birthday. Whatever had happened, those years were now irretrievably lost, the girl had gone forever and, if still alive, a woman existed.

Sister Diane, happily married and living in North Norfolk, had two daughters and maintained her close family ties, as did Pamela who had added a daughter to the son that April had happily wheeled through Roughton so long ago. The proud parents and grandparents could only sadly speculate upon the family role that April might have filled.

No longer could there be hope of restoration and a renewed unaffected happiness. A large chunk of evolving family life had gone; restoration would start at a new point, if it became possible. Twenty years had ravaged police optimism, almost eliminated public expectation, and dulled family hopes. Only dulled – they still existed.

Albert Fabb pointed out, 'You mustn't give up hope. It will keep you going.'

Olive Fabb agreed, saying, 'You never know if someone might admit they took April away.'

The police refused to give up, to consign the case to history. The retiring head of CID visited the parents to promise that even though police officers may come and go, the case endured. He advised them of his successor, wished them well and retired to other interests, which several years later were to incorporate this account.

The new head of Norfolk CID, Detective Chief Superintendent Alan Smith, came to post without previous involvement in the case, as had the head of CID before him. Like his predecessor he introduced himself and fielded the regular enquiries and information that still surfaced, mostly from dreamers and the psychic brigade. On the twentieth anniversary he made a renewed effort by publicising the case again, calling a press conference at North Walsham Police Station. If his non-involvement in the original enquiries was a potential hindrance to the conference it was smartly solved by inviting back the officer in the case. Reg Lester came out of retirement.

More effect was created by inviting April's parents. Distressing as it must have been for the plucky couple, they never refused an opportunity to reach out to those who might help, repeating their agonised plea for information; the same plea that had fallen on stony ground for so many years. They never gave up, whatever the price in an acceleration of their private, now public, grief.

The clock was turned back as Reg Lester was reunited with April's parents to re-create the twenty years old case, projecting yet again the facts of Norfolk's greatest mystery. The ex-detective stated quite firmly that the case would never end until April returned to her parents or police discovered what had happened to her.

*Figure 9.1 Reg Lester returns from retirement to sit next to
Mr and Mrs Fabb at the 1989 press conference.*
Archant (Norfolk)

Alan Smith explained, before the conference started, 'There's
nothing new: it's simply the fact it's twenty years on.'

He summarised the saga of April Fabb, saying, 'We have never been
off the Fabb case. It has continually come to the top over the years.'

During the course of the conference he encapsulated police
feelings, saying, 'There are other missing person cases but this one
does not go away and I don't want it to.'

It was well put. He appealed to the public to solve the long standing
riddle.

Albert and Olive Fabb had not refused an interview or a baulked at
a question over twenty years. At the conference they gave measured
answers of great sincerity, delivered with the same quiet dignity that
had attended every other meeting with the police and the public.
Quietly they spoke to the world, giving a simple heartrending plea:
'Please help us discover what happened to our daughter.'

Time had not eroded the parents' quest, or their belief that one day
it would end with the truth.

Mrs Fabb told the conference, 'I still hope that April might be found one day. Until they find her body I cling to the hope that she is still alive. I have to do that to keep myself going.'

With the single minded devotion of a mother grieving the unexplained absence of a daughter, she told the hushed gathering, 'I can't be turned away from my belief that she will come home. Time has healed us a little, but she is on our minds every single day.'

Mr Fabb answered questions that had changed very little over twenty years. He took a more forthright view.

'I don't think she could be still alive,' he said. 'I have come to the conclusion that if she wasn't abducted she would have come home on the day she went out on that cycle ride.'

The aim of the conference was to re-introduce a partly new public to the facts, to re-identify the pathos and trauma of the long running mystery. Reg Lester contributed with his own reminder that police officers are human, bringing to a newly attentive public a phrase that had travelled from 1969, and was still applicable.

He said, 'I would like to side with Mrs Fabb and hold out some hope for April. I still think about the case every day, because someone, somewhere, must know what happened.' As true as the day he first spoke it.

Figure 9.2 1993 and renewed publicity.
Archant (Norfolk)

Whoever that someone was had granite like emotions, if the publicised conference found its mark. The result was opinions and dreamers – nothing tangible; on into the 1990s without any new light.

The passing years, the new decade, did not bring anonymity for the Fabb family. They were always liable to be engaged in conversation by well meaning but unproductive gossipers who wished to comment or sympathise. Some were undiplomatic enough to tender unfounded opinions, even profess knowledge, such as the elderly shopper who sagely informed Olive Fabb of the whereabouts, vaguely given, of the man responsible for taking April, a view that garnered little or no substance and owed more to the shopper's advanced years than genuine knowledge.

More anniversaries, more interest and information, but no progress! Then, within a month of the twenty-fifth anniversary (noted in the press without great exclamation), a television producer and crew arrived in Norfolk to interview the police and the Fabbs. (They were also interested in the compilation of this book).

Mr and Mrs Fabb had seen many television producers over the years and this lot seemed no different. The elderly couple co-operated, as they had always done, and even agreed to re-visit Metton where they posed in the churchyard with nostalgic views of number 3 Council Houses and, with devastating poignancy, in Back Lane at the point where April had disappeared. Many years earlier Mrs Fabb had stood at this same spot at the behest of a national newspaper reporter, now here she was again, looking at a grassy bank framing a ploughed field, under towering trees, contemplating and suffering the unknown circumstances that had taken her daughter from this very place.

The day was taken up with more pictures, some posed on Cromer pier, interviews in a room crowded with a television crew and a carefully watching detective, and much discussion that was not for the programme. It was too much and Olive Fabb dissolved into tears. So much, over so long, with no result! Would there ever be an end? Possibly! This television producer had not been prompted by the urge or command to mark an anniversary, or present yet another documentary of mystery for general edification. This producer had travelled from Yorkshire because of the belief, supported by the product of similar facts, that April had been abducted and murdered. And the murderer was in custody, or so it was thought.

It began in 1990, on a hot July afternoon (a familiar scenario). A retired man tended his garden in another England/Scotland border village, at the same time idly watching a young girl walking towards a parked van. As she walked behind the van only her feet were visible, until they suddenly disappeared upwards. She had been scooped into the van, which then drove away.

The witness moved quickly, noting the van number and ringing the police. Without doubt he saved the girl's life. The police were quickly on the scene, with the girl's father, and, astonishingly, as the witness was briefing them, the van reappeared. The police stopped the vehicle and grabbed the driver. The girl was in the back, tied up, sexually assaulted – but alive. The killer of Susan Maxwell, Caroline Hogg and Sarah Harper was in police hands.

It was four years before the police proved the three murders against their prisoner; four years during which Robert Black refused to answer questions on the cases, even though he had no hope of release. The judge had recognised the full depravity and implication of the crime for which he had been arrested, and to which he pleaded 'Guilty', and sentenced him to life imprisonment. His convictions four years later for the murders of Susan Maxwell, Caroline Hogg and Sarah Harper resulted in further life sentences, a triumph for police persistence.

At his murder trial in 1994 Black spoke only twice, officially. He confirmed his name and said he was not guilty. After the verdicts of 'Guilty' he looked at the police officers and murmured, 'Well done boys.' And indeed they had done well. Four years of intensive investigation convicted him of the three murders, also an attempted abduction of a fifteen years old girl in the suburbs of Nottingham in 1988 when he had been interrupted in the act of forcing her into his van.

Unsolved abductions and murders in Britain, Ireland and France were checked against Black's known movements. Suspicion because of what he was, what he had done, but suspicion without proof. April Fabb from Norfolk, Christine Markham from Scunthorpe and Genette Tate from Devon were looked at, among others. Some reports put Black in Devon on the day in 1978 that Genette disappeared. There was nothing to place him in Norfolk at any time, and Humberside police later identified a much stronger suspect for the murder of Christine Markham, a man they could not interview because he had died.

Silence tends to attract suspicion of matters to which a person might rightly say he was innocent. But then, serial offenders who are convicted and remain in denial inevitably inspire questions concerning the extent of their guilt.

Pocock, Hopkins and Black! And there would be more. Was April's fate bound to such a person?

Sufficient Conclusions from Insufficient Premises

The church visitor has travelled far in a travelogue of knowledge, curiosity, sympathy and hope, but it nears an end that was known from the start. An interim ending awaiting a real ending, which must be the final chapter, as yet unwritten – the truth of April Fabb's going and the place where she is now.

The reader who has lasted the journey, now thirty-eight years, has been apprised of the relevant facts, and - in hindsight - perhaps several not so relevant, and is in a position to decide the most likely answer to this enduring mystery.

Perhaps a particular reader knows the answer because he is the 'someone, somewhere' - the cycle thrower in Back Lane in 1969.

Perhaps a knowledgeable reader is merely an agent of that knowledge, an acquirer as opposed to a perpetrator, resting uncomfortably with the guilt of another.

Questions! Are there apparent answers? A British writer of the nineteenth century said, 'Life is the art of drawing sufficient conclusions from insufficient premises.' The premises have been identified along the journey taken by the reader. Now it is time to judge where the truth is likely to lie. And if the reader actually knows then let compassion be seen and the family be told.

The first assessment required from the known facts is: what happened? Then: who? And where is April now? If the case is solved by the time of reading, or the still hidden truth is known to the reader, the incorrect can be noted with the correct.

History cannot of course be rewritten, although some may try. Even if all were now revealed the tragedy is already confirmed, an irreversible process of many years that cannot be recalled with a new script of happiness. Nothing can repay the grief of the Fabb family; no result or conclusion can alter the past; but a new form of happiness is possible after all this time.

The future can bring satisfaction, a triumph of faith, relief in the receipt of knowledge that can lead to reunification with April, even if it is with the realisation of death; then at least there can be a known place and a recognised bereavement replacing the tortured speculation of so many years. Mrs Fabb speaks of a traffic accident with an almost longing voice, pointing out they would have had a recognisable incident, a tangible known circumstance that had removed a loved one yet returned her for mourning and memoriam. The parents that brought her into the world would have known the manner of her going and grieved accordingly. Instead, they have grieved for a vacuum that swallowed their child without explanation.

Figure 10.1 The last known picture of April, part of the film of a school trip

The parents have never sought revenge, neither have they looked for exactly the same result as the police. They wished to know. They wished to be reunited with their daughter. The identity of the person who inflicted so much misery upon them is incidental, of great importance to the police but never tied to thoughts of vengeance or retribution by Albert and Olive Fabb. They dealt with this point in a very simple and practical way: it is done, it cannot be undone. Let there be a coming to terms with the result, achieved only with knowledge of what happened and where April is now.

So far there has been nothing beyond facts and circumstantial evidence indicating a meeting and confrontation in Back Lane. What kind of meeting and confrontation?

It is presumed that the attentive reader will discount any pre-arranged or contrived meeting between April and a person she knew. A meeting, yes! But not of her making. The sequence and logic of the perceived facts rules out the possibility that April engineered her disappearance. So how did the meeting come about?

A vehicle approached and stopped – certainly; from what direction? Is the direction of the vehicle indicated by the circumstances?

It is likely that a male driver stopped, motivated by the isolation, beautiful weather, and the slowly moving pretty girl ahead. If he approached April from behind, from Pillar Box Corner, he would have had plenty of time to view her and make a calculated decision to overtake and pull in front or alongside her. There was no evidence of a collision or accident in any form, and the straightness and length of the road would have given the driver sufficient thinking time before reaching the slowly moving cyclist in front of him, a cyclist who may have been pushing her cycle in deference to the warm weather and uphill slope. His decision was to stop in a place where there is no normal reason to stop. April was the reason for stopping. He had formed an intention.

Some awkwardness attends this approach from the rear. If the driver approached April in the same direction as her travel he would have overtaken or come upon her on his nearside, presuming she was keeping to her left (her cycle was thrown to that side). That would make the width of his vehicle an obstruction between him and the girl (presuming right-hand drive) and the bank on which he probably stood to throw the cycle. (If hurled from the road it was a prodigious throw).

Driving from the opposite direction, from Roughton head-on towards April, a driver would be over the brow of the hill and seeing her no more than one hundred yards ahead. From this direction stopping would have been a quick decision, but opening the driver's door would have been sufficient to bar the girl's forward progress in the narrow lane. He would have been immediately alongside the grassy bank, and April.

Whatever direction he appeared from, whether he ran round, back or forward from his vehicle, or stepped out alongside April, what happened next was known to only two, possibly three, persons. Did he entice, threaten or physically force her into the vehicle? Was there conversation or just a fast and furious propulsion? Perhaps the driver asked for directions or offered a lift as a prelude to capturing her. Perhaps he made his intentions plain from the outset. A possibility not to be overlooked is that he had seen her earlier, maybe even seen her leave the donkey field. We just do not know.

Whatever the chronicle of events, time would be of the essence. A driver disposed to kidnapping would not wish to delay in a road that could produce another vehicle. Back Lane was not wide enough for passing traffic.

Was the cycle thrown into the field after April had been placed in the vehicle? Or was she a witness to the man standing on the grassy bank pitching her cycle several feet into the ploughed field? Such an act would have, by its finality, revealed a terrible intent. Does this question suggest the presence of two attackers? It should be remembered that April was shy, reserved to the point of nervousness with strangers, and could well have been terrified into silence and immobility by one person. She was stranded in a landscape of nothing, vulnerable, exposed, and without any visible form of rescue. Even if she screamed, and it seems she did not, who would have heard her? She had no knowledge of two dozing picnickers and four dogs in Tom Tit Lane.

Was the cycle thrown as a demonstration that the young girl had no means of escape, or to remove an indicator to her abduction?

That the vehicle driver was known to April cannot be discounted. Indeed, this intriguing question has exercised many minds, spawned several theories and speculative suspects. The disposal of the cycle suggests swift and determined action with a minimum of dialogue.

Pitching the cycle over the bank into Three Corner Field left it exposed to the view of traffic on the Cromer road, and indeed it was quickly seen – seemingly within minutes, perhaps seconds, of the pitching. Throwing the cycle over the opposite bank would have left it unseen, liable to be found only by persons searching the area – and that would have been many hours later. Conclusions may be drawn from this choice of throwing sides, if it was choice as opposed to impulse. In a fast moving incident circumstances may have dictated the disposal of the cycle.

How long did the confrontation last? Minutes? Seconds? It will be recalled that at a reconstructed time of two-six pm April was seen approaching Pillar Box Corner. The point in Back Lane from where her cycle was thrown is unlikely to be less than two minutes or more than four minutes away from that point, depending how slowly she cycled uphill that warm day. Accordingly, the confrontation occurred at about two-eight/nine or two-ten pm. Her cycle was spotted in the field at two-fifteen. The recollection of her friends, however, is that she left the donkey field at two-ten pm or just after, which makes an abduction time almost coincidental with the time the cycle was seen in the field, provided of course that time is spot-on.

Times given by witnesses, whether arrived at by recollection or reconstruction, must inevitably have some elasticity. For instance, at two-six pm she is by one account approaching Pillar Box Corner and by another she is still in the donkey field, not leaving there until around two-ten. These two places are about a minute, maybe a minute and half, apart by cycle ride. Allowing a margin of error on proffered times of a few minutes (not many persons can time themselves exactly in a given day), the sequence is broadly revealing. April vanished in or around the two-ten to two-fifteen time bracket; very quickly!

The very narrow time frame of April's disappearance has been deduced from witnesses who saw much, but not enough. As some have said – 'it is as if she had just been lifted up into the sky'. And there were those who spoke of UFOs! (After Genette Tate's disappearance searchers found by an area of scorched grass in the field near to her abandoned cycle, exciting UFO enthusiasts, less so the police who said that, while they would not rule anything out, a farmer's over-zealous use of nitrogen fertiliser seemed a more likely answer).

Returning to the compelling question of whether the driver was known to April, it has been suggested on several occasions, usually by people drawn into the remote countryside around Metton for the first time, that only a person with knowledge of the area would have been in Back Lane. Maybe, but holiday areas do attract explorers, it was the aftermath of Easter, drivers do get lost, and there are other motives for driving along new roads, however uninviting. Frank, the Norwich crook furiously driving his van past the Council Houses, was one example. A predatory, searching, prospective kidnapper cannot be beyond reason, exampled by later cases.

Was the abducting vehicle a van? Such a proposition makes sense yet may not be true if the driver acted upon impulse. A car is a mobile greenhouse in terms of visibility, not apparently suitable for abducting people, yet Pocock used one – a Volvo estate, and kept the Cambridgeshire schoolgirls inside for many hours. And cars in 1969 did not project the glass area of their modern counterparts.

Non sequitur [the answer does not follow the evidence] can apply. The truth may defy the evidence. The detective's rationality may not be that of the criminal's. But is there scope for defining April's disappearance other than as an impromptu and swift abduction? Apparently not! And the motive? We do not know but a presumption can be drawn from other cases examined in this book.

In our assumed abduction we have a man, a vehicle and a place, and possible directions of travel to that place. A very important point is the direction of travel from that place, surely dictated by the direction of arrival. The sequence of known events may now be related to a getaway vehicle.

Travelling from Roughton into Back Lane (the opposite direction to April) the kidnapping vehicle was unseen. But after the abduction driving through Metton created possibilities, and one of the girls in the donkey field did recall the builder's van going past 'not long after April left'. In fact, that particular van did not go past for another half hour, a time well remembered because it was nearly in collision with the Norwich crook's van. Two possibilities! The van *was* the builder's van and the time lapse was greater than recalled, or another van – with April inside.

There were sequences that avoided a getaway vehicle journeying through the potential witness territory of Metton after leaving Back Lane: turning at Pillar Box Corner towards Hanworth, a rarely used even narrower lane, or a U turn into the Cromer road towards Felbrigg. A kidnapper, however, probably just sought to distance himself from the scene as quickly as possible. If he was facing the direction of April's travel he would be in Roughton and on the main Norwich-Cromer road within minutes. Whatever route the vehicle containing April took, the luck that attended the kidnapping was continued. His luck, not April's!

If the reader is not dizzy with geographical conjecture there is an even more interesting route to ponder over, that taken by the Land Rover driver who saw April approaching Pillar Box Corner at the reconstructed time of two–six pm. He was travelling in the opposite direction, into Metton. Her movement to the point where her cycle was found would more than equal the time taken by his progress through Metton, therefore: if the vehicle that captured April came through Metton to approach her from behind it must have passed the Land Rover. The result of this equation is a grey car and a red Mini with new reflective number plates. Neither was traced.

Who was the driver who stopped alongside April? What was he? Applying the doctrine of similar facts and the civil test of a preponderance of probabilities, April was unfortunate enough to meet a man of Pocock, Hopkins or Black type. A predatory stranger! This, whilst likely, cannot be proved and the local knowledge theory, and possibility of a confrontation with somebody she knew, should not be discounted. Whoever she met, the evidence weighs heavily towards a sudden confrontation, brief interaction and fast escape.

The police could not connect Pocock, Hopkins (only twelve years old at the time) or Black with the April Fabb case, though they continued to wonder whether these men retained other terrible secrets. Police officers become suspicious doubting persons by reason of their trade, something to do with the persistent receipt of untruths and a frequent contact with those whom the general law-abiding public would rather not meet. They are also inclined to proceed under the premise that criminals are not always apprehended on the occasion of their first crime. Such reasoning does raise the thought provoking assumption that whoever kidnapped April had already committed similar offences and would go on to commit more offences, until caught.

Many have queried whether Robert Black abducted April Fabb, the question motivated by the heavily publicised horror of his crimes against young girls. If he did the evidence is missing. Black was twenty-two years of age in 1969, born and raised in Scotland but moving to London in late 1968 or early 1969. He worked as a swimming pool attendant and part-time barman but did not possess a driving licence until the mid-seventies (though convicted of driving offences in 1972). If he had access to, or drove a vehicle in 1969, or strayed from working and drinking in London in that year, it is not a matter of record or knowledge. After obtaining his driving licence he became employed as a long distance van driver, a job that put him in the wrong place for three young girls in the 1980s.

Figure 10.2 The police file is still open.
Copyright of Norfolk Constabulary

Black had a disturbing sexual history in Scotland, mostly as a child and youth, but his name missed the trawl instigated by the Maxwell and Hogg investigations. They looked for known *serious* sexual offenders, senior officers believing that seeking names of *all* sex offenders would have swamped the inquiry. It is a salutary thought that if his name had been projected, as happened with Pocock and Hopkins in 1985, he would probably have been captured earlier. Intelligence is the key, but only if it is known and shared.

The stargazers, dreamers and the like might wish to make something out of Black's birthday of 21 April, with April Fabb's occurring on 22 April, but there has been much postulation on indistinct, unproven sciences and beliefs and if there is any connection between these two persons, beyond similar facts enhanced by press speculation, it has yet to be revealed. All sorts of coincidences may be drawn without advancing a conclusion.

Black has not been implicated in the disappearance of April Fabb, neither has he been eliminated from the inquiry. If he was responsible where does April now lie? And will he ever tell? Only the person who took April can answer these questions. Black delivered the sad little bodies of Susan, Caroline and Sarah into the area that became known as the 'Midlands Triangle', using his regular employment as a van driver. He was so employed when Genette Tate disappeared in 1978. Not so in 1969 when April Fabb disappeared.

Black is not scheduled for release before 2029 and one has to wonder who will, even then, dare make the decision to release him. In 2005 he was taken to Northern Ireland and interviewed concerning the murder of Jennifer Cardy. In this same year the Devon and Cornwall Constabulary interviewed him concerning the disappearance of Genette Tate. The evidence justifying these interviews, and Black's response, with the result of enquiries up to 2007, are pending legal opinion.*

In the cases involving Pocock and Hopkins the victims were moved 70 miles. Jane Taylor was taken 100 miles. Black's victims were taken as far as 300 miles. What chance did April's two miles radius search have? And if she has been murdered and buried what chance is there of discovery, even now? Is she liable to be found through the spread of urbanisation, new buildings and complexes taking over the countryside, or by the off-road explorations of ramblers, naturalists, archaeologists and the like? She could be hidden on private property. And the sea is only a few miles from Metton. A matter of note is that Black sought to dispose of his victims rather than consciously hide them. A questionable point if he has other victims, unfound!

A provocative thought, touched upon earlier: how many perverts, sexual assaulters, kidnappers and murderers fail to come to notice and continually avoid detection in their compulsive, continuing catalogue of offences? They pursue their predatory urges until arrested and removed from the public arena, then disappearing into the segregated confines of prison custody still retaining other dark secrets. If April's kidnapper is of that kind then he is known to the police somewhere, for something.

None of the assembled hypotheses proves that April is not still in Norfolk, the victim of a random circumstance perpetrated by a once only, never to be repeated impulse. Neither does the projection of similar facts prove that April is dead, the victim of crime. The reader will judge on what is known.

---

* Readers wishing to research further into the life and times of Robert Black are recommended to *'The Murder of Childhood'* by *Ray Wyre*, also *'Fear the Stranger'* by *Hector Clark (retired Deputy Chief Constable of Lothian and Borders)*.

Whichever way the balance of knowledge points there is a shortage of the most precious information of all: defining evidence. If Mrs Fabb says that April is alive somewhere, even now, there is no evidence to say she is wrong. Improbable and inconsistent as it is with the sequence of events, the known facts and the applied reasoning, it is not disproved. If a prayer could resolve the mystery of thirty-eight years it would be that she is right. The visitor to St Andrew's Church would, before leaving with newfound knowledge, make that prayer, at the same time acknowledging that thirty-eight years have been irretrievably lost.

Epilogue

Behold, I shew you a mystery; We shall not all sleep,
But we shall all be changed.　　Corinthians 15.51

The 1995 epilogue has become a stage in the sad process of time that is the April Fabb story, and its opening paragraph is now a preface the 2007 epilogue.

'The small bungalow nestles decoratively below the level of the adjoining road, masked by carefully tended plants, framed in the quiet stillness of a short cul-de-sac. Sunlight glances through the trellis climbing clematis, probing the compact, immaculately kept living room, revealing comfortable furniture and proudly displayed mementoes of the elderly occupiers. The focal point, the television, carries a delicately framed photograph centred on a background of soft pink roses. Both photograph and roses are prominent and permanent. April Fabb looks at her parents every day and every day they think of her, and wonder.'

Albert and Olive Fabb waited and hoped; but time can be cruel to those who seek a deserved happiness.

In 1995 the Fabb family tempered the agony of the unknown with a focal point for their bereavement, a permanent marker for them and the outside world, superseding a notice pinned to a church door. A memorial headstone in St Andrew's churchyard would forever proclaim who April Fabb was, and the mystery of her going. The family asked that the wording of the notice on the church door be repeated, words that had lasted on paper for so many years and would now be inscribed in stone. Where to place the memorial? April's sisters had no doubt! It should stand at the very spot where April always stood with her friends chatting after Sunday School: in the recess next to the church entrance. And so it stands, April's place, facing the path and the gate, viewed by all who enter the church.

On a sunny September day Albert and Olive Fabb made tearful progress along the church path to view the memorial for the first time, followed by Pamela and Diane. Serious faced spectators stood back in respectful silence. A watching writer noted the tears and wondered. Should this splendid family have been left with their memories, resigned to a seemingly unsolvable mystery? Assurance followed that the Fabbs would never give up their quest for knowledge, however distressing the road might be. Only death would end their determination. And now they had a special place to go to, a place where April's name was irrevocably carved. And who was to say the mystery of her going was not solvable?

The dedication and blessing of April's memorial by the Reverend Keith James was an emotional occasion. Inside the packed church, his voice broken by the occasion, the reverend preached to a hushed congregation, telling of 'a little candle burning with the pure clear light of joy and laughter', and the 'greater darkness' of 'the unknowing, the uncertainty'. He told April's parents 'You know, as only parents can, just who she was. And one day you will know what happened.' Twenty-six years on from the happy days in 1969, when April placed flowers in the church, he was speaking to a forest of faces strained by sorrow and the memory of a near fourteen years old girl. There was no conception of a forty years old woman. The complete sermon can be found as an appendix to this book.

Tragedy continued to stalk the Fabb family. In 1997 Bernard, husband of Pamela and the brother-in-law April had fatefully journeyed to visit with her present on 8 April 1969, died, aged only fifty-six years. In 1998 Albert Ernest Fabb died, never knowing in this world what happened to his youngest daughter. This pleasantly resolute and uncomplicated man, admired and respected by all who knew him, and knew of him, was devoid of bitterness for the inhumanity of other men. He and his family deserved the knowledge they never realised. His funeral took place at St Andrew's Church, Metton on 2 April and one of his hymns was 'Lord of all Hopefulness'. His ashes are interred under a tablet in front of April's memorial. Reunited in spirit!

As the twentieth century neared its end without resolution of the mystery the facts remained no less intriguing to police, public and the media. Information, suggestions and just openly declared interest continued to surface, and that interest reached far beyond the United

Kingdom. A new twist on false trails occurred in September 1998 when an American woman travelled from Los Angeles to Norfolk, recalling a vague history as a child in eastern England. She believed she might be April Fabb, and indeed she was of an appropriate age – in itself a reminder of the years that had been lost. Whoever she was she was not April Fabb, proved by police enquiries and technology undreamed of in 1969 – DNA!

In 2007 new information is still recorded, some fatuous and speculative, some interesting and worthy of enquiry but ultimately unproductive. The last message to the police from a member of the public concerning April arrived only the week before the penning of this epilogue. There will have been others before the reading of this sad story.

Today Diane and Pamela are mothers and grandmothers, and Diane's daughter and granddaughter have the memorable middle name of April. Two sisters grieve and wonder but their photographs and mementoes ensure that their younger sister is never far away.

Olive Fabb lives in Cromer with her own photographs and mementoes; she is elderly and alert, stoically mindful of personal tragedy, undiminished in her faith and desire for the truth. She has been truly described as an amazing lady. Pamela and Diane continue to live in North Norfolk and the family remain close in mind, spirit and practice. They no longer have to regularly fend against intruding media, insensitive and unexpected visitors and the 'revelations' of stargazers, dreamers, dowsers and psychics; just an occasional enquiry and a lone writer, to whom they have extended the utmost courtesy. They did receive an invitation to view the paintings of a Norwich artist who, fascinated, as so many have been, by the mystery, produced a series of pictures inspired by 'The Lost Years'. The writer received a similar invitation and viewed them thinking how far in interest, and how long in time, the mystery of April Fabb had reached.

Police officers have come and gone. The April Fabb file has not gone! It is not closed! It never was! Some officers examining the file today were not born when April took her last journey and nearly all in the Norfolk force are younger than April would be today, but there is no time closure to her investigation. The Norfolk Constabulary remains responsive to information, which still arrives. Reg Lester and colleagues long retired still ponder. The family of April Fabb, and the county of Norfolk, still wait.

A corner of a churchyard that is forever April's

Appendix

Sermon preached by the Reverend Keith James
in St Andrew's Church, Metton, 3 September 1995

'In his book 'The Lost Years' Maurice Morson states that the story of April Fabb is 'a story awaiting an ending'.

It was just that as I sat drinking coffee with my colleagues in the Dental Practice in Prince of Wales Road in Norwich after the Easter break in 1969; clearly I remember our questioning, our discussion. Patient after patient coming in with that same question on their lips. What has happened to April Fabb?

It was just such a story waiting an ending today. The yearning, the searching, the heartache and the longing, the detective work goes on. Today as we remember April and proudly yet sadly look at the simple stone which stands as a sign of grief mingled with faint hope we may have come to the end of a chapter, but the story remains unfinished; the book of life – or death – lies open.

For most of us, however deep our interest, and our concern, it is a 'story.' As Reg Lester has written, for us 'the harrowing emptiness in the life of a caring family and the added strain of the countless years of 'not knowing' is too difficult to contemplate.

To us it is a story, something in the daily papers; but to you it has been real.

The little candle burning with the pure clear light of joy and laughter and the chatter and naughtiness and likes and dislikes that shone in this small corner known as Metton became a victim of the many kinds of darkness that are found in the world.

Perhaps the greater darkness has been the unknowing, the uncertainty. And you have known in your hearts too the darkness of despair. A grieving for the years you hoped for, the expectations you had, for this your child, your sister, your friend.

The darkness too perhaps of times of anger, even guilt – feelings made all the darker because we feel they should not be there, but of course they are.

Darkness again as each year has rolled on, each birthday, each anniversary of that awful day in 1969 had come and gone with still no word.

You have indeed smarted for what is a little while in God's eyes, but in human terms seems an eternity.

You have passed through the assayer's fire, and you have stood the test. I want to make it quite clear that I do not believe that the trials you have endured, far less the misfortune that befell your April, were sent by God to test you.

But I do believe in a God who has shared your anguish with you, and who has given you the strength to live with that strange mixture of acceptance of the probability that April died a child and the faint hope that she lived to be a woman and would one day come walking up the path.

Whatever happened, however dim now the light that was April, you have kept her alive. Alive in your hearts, alive in remembrance, alive in your prayers. The light still shines.

That light will now shine on after you have gone; who knows how many years, how many centuries, the stone outside will last. Who knows how many will read the inscription, and wonder, not just what happened, but who was April?

You know as only parents can just who she was. And one day you will know what happened.

For as Christians we believe we have an inheritance that is kept for us in the mystery of heaven. And you, because you have put your faith in God, are under the protection of his power. In that power shall all things be revealed in Christ.

That same Jesus Christ who said 'Let the children come to me', and put his arms around them, and blessed them holds your April in His love, waiting to reunite you.

Praise be to the God and Father of our Lord Jesus Christ, who in his great mercy gives us new birth in a living hope – the hope of an end to the uncertainty, the end of the Lost Years, a closing of the final chapter, and a new beginning together in the life to come.'

Reproduced by kind permission of the Reverend Keith James

Index

A140, 16,
Aldborough, 46
Amen Corner/Lowe, 22
Australia, 60,103
Aylesbeare, 97,98
Aylmerton, 16,21
Aylsham, 18,68,76,87

B1436, 16,29,67,69
Back Lane, 16,18,20,23,26,29,31,33,36,
    37,42,44,66,69,70,90,92,111,116,119,
    122-124
Baconsthorpe, 25
Bacton, 83
Banningham, 105
Bass, Dick, D/Sgt, 44,49,50,58
Bedfordshire, 111,112
Bernard, brother-in-law, 21,23-27,34,
    35,130
Black, Robert,117,118,125-127
Blakeney, 82
Bradwell, 101
British T/Police, 47

Cambridge(shire), 108-110,124
Cardy, Jennifer, 100,127
Cheshire, 78,92,106
Chiddick, P/C, 33-35
Christine, friend, 25,30
Clark, Hector, 127
Cockley Cley, 94,100
Council Houses,18-20,24,29,35,37,
    57,61,63,67,81,106,107,116,123
Cromer, 14-16,18,20-23,25-27,29,31-33,
    35,37,38,41,42,45-48,56,60,65-68,70,
    73,86,101,102,106,107,116,122,124,
    131
Cromer Police Station, 33,35,48,99,
    101,106
Cromer School, 21,59,99
Croydon, 82
Curls' store, 60

Dersingham, 94
Devon, 97,98,105,117,127
Downham Market, 95
Duncan, nephew, 21,23,78
Dye, John, D/Insp, 44,45,101

East Runton, 22,59
Edinburgh, 108
Empson, David, 26,33,49,50,72-74
Erpingham, 81
Essex, 111
Exall, Pamela, 93-95,97,100
Exeter, 98
Exmouth, 98

Fabb, Albert, from 20,
    April, from 10
    Diane, from 20
    Olive, from 20
    Pamela, from 20
Fakenham, 77
Felbrigg, 16,26,29,31,52,56,59,67,70,
    80,124
France, 117
Francis, P/Sgt, 37
Frank, suspect, 68,74,123
Fulbourn, 109
Gillian, friend, 22,24,26-28,34,35
Great Wood, 52
Great Yarmouth, 39,101,111,112
Gresham, 16,18,26,31
Guildford, 82
Gunton Park, 51

Hall Farm, 18,22-24,26,31,70
Hampshire, 60
Hanworth, 46,70,124
Harper, Sarah, 112,117,126
Harrison, farmer, 22,23,26,70,107
Hazelend, 85
Hellesdon Hospital, 90
Hertfordshire, 106
Hogg, Caroline, 108,109,112,117,126
Holland, 76,82
HOLMES,101,102,108,110,111
Hopkins, Gary, 111,112,118,124-127
House of Commons, 63
Humberside, 117

Ipswich, 111
Ireland, 100,117,127

James, Rev Keith, 130,133,134
Jane, friend, 24
Jenkins, Roy, 58
Jersey, 106

Kelling Heath, 51
Kings Lynn, 95

Lancashire, 91
Leeds, 112
Leicester(shire), 82,108
Leoni, 111
Lester, Reg, D/C/Supt, 38,41-45,53,
    58,59,62-64,75,77,83,87-91,97,99-101,
    106,113-115,131,133
Lincolnshire, 92
Long, Susan, 87-89,95,100
London, 40,47,95,125
Los Angeles, 131
Lothian & Borders Police, 108,109
Lowe, Andy F, 22

Manchester, 60
Markham, Christine, 92,94,97,117
Matlaske, 105
Maureen, friend, 30
Maxwell, Susan, 108,109,112,117,126
Member/ Parliament, 63,81
Met' Police, 39
Metton,10,16,18,19,21,22,26,27,29,31,
    33-35,46,48,57,60,66-71,86,87,91,97,
    99,107,116,123-125,127,130
Middle East, 106
Mildenhall, 111
MIRIAM, 101,102

New Scotland Yard, 38-41,87,88,95
Newing, Steven, 77,94,95,97,100
Newmarket, 80
Nixon, Richard, 58
Norfolk Constabulary, 11,39,60,108,131
Norfolk Joint Police, 39,42,51
North Wales, 78
North Walsham, 26,37,41,42,44,45,47,
    56,70,113
Northrepps, 16,22,24
Northumbria, 108,109
Norwich, 16,21,23,26-28,37-39,44,47,
    55,56,60,65,68,74,87,90,110,124,131
Norwich Airport, 104
Norwich Police, 41
Norwich Prison, 89,90
Nottingham, 112,117

Ostend, 82
Overstrand, 24
Oxford, 82

Pillar Box Corner,16,18,26,31,33,36,50,
    66,71,74,86,121,123,124
Pipeline, 46,55,67,83
Pocock, Terence, 110-112,118,124-127
Potter Heigham, 82
Pretty Corner, 51,89-91

RAF, 46,51
Reddin, Heidi, 95,97
Rockland St Mary, 91
Roughton, 16,21,23,24,29,33-35,42,46,
    48,57,59,66-70,113,121,124

Scotland, 108,117,125,126
Scunthorpe, 92,117
Sheringham, 14,16,89,90
Sidmouth, 98
Sizewell, 104
Smith, Alan, D/C/Supt,113,114
Snettisham, 93
Southampton, 104
Staffordshire, 108
Stalham, 81
St Andrew's Church, 19,29,60,79,93,
    128-130,133
Stiffkey Marshes, 91
Stourbridge, 82
Suffolk, 108,111
Susan, friend, 22-26,27,30,35,78
Sustead, 18,26,32,34,35,46,57,66,70-74
Swansea, 92

Tangiers, 82
Tate, Genette, 97-100,105,117,123,127
Taylor, Jane, 78,92,94,97,106,127
Taylor, Reg, D/C/Insp, 45,57,63,89,101
Thetford Forest, 109,110
Three Corner Field, 16,26,50,122
Tom Tit Lane, 26,32,66,122
Toulouse, 82
Trudy, April's dog, 22-25,61,78,106
Twycross, 108

Uttoxeter/Stafford Road, 108

Victoria Bus/Station, 47,56,60

Walsall, 41
Wilson, Harold, 58
Wisbech, 81
Woodgate, 85
Wyre, Ray, 127

Yorkshire, 102,103,116